T0091839

MARITIME SECURITY

Protection of Marinas, Ports,
Small Watercraft, Yachts, and Ships

MARITIME SECURITY

Protection of Marinas, Ports, Small Watercraft, Yachts, and Ships

Daniel J. Benny, Ph.D.

CRC Press
Taylor & Francis Group
Boca Raton London New York

CRC Press is an imprint of the
Taylor & Francis Group, an **informa** business

CRC Press
Taylor & Francis Group
6000 Broken Sound Parkway NW, Suite 300
Boca Raton, FL 33487-2742

© 2016 by Taylor & Francis Group, LLC
CRC Press is an imprint of Taylor & Francis Group, an Informa business

No claim to original U.S. Government works

Printed on acid-free paper
Version Date: 20150721

International Standard Book Number-13: 978-1-4987-0660-5 (Hardback)

This book contains information obtained from authentic and highly regarded sources. Reasonable efforts have been made to publish reliable data and information, but the author and publisher cannot assume responsibility for the validity of all materials or the consequences of their use. The authors and publishers have attempted to trace the copyright holders of all material reproduced in this publication and apologize to copyright holders if permission to publish in this form has not been obtained. If any copyright material has not been acknowledged please write and let us know so we may rectify in any future reprint.

Except as permitted under U.S. Copyright Law, no part of this book may be reprinted, reproduced, transmitted, or utilized in any form by any electronic, mechanical, or other means, now known or hereafter invented, including photocopying, microfilming, and recording, or in any information storage or retrieval system, without written permission from the publishers.

For permission to photocopy or use material electronically from this work, please access www.copyright.com (http://www.copyright.com/) or contact the Copyright Clearance Center, Inc. (CCC), 222 Rosewood Drive, Danvers, MA 01923, 978-750-8400. CCC is a not-for-profit organization that provides licenses and registration for a variety of users. For organizations that have been granted a photocopy license by the CCC, a separate system of payment has been arranged.

Trademark Notice: Product or corporate names may be trademarks or registered trademarks, and are used only for identification and explanation without intent to infringe.

Visit the Taylor & Francis Web site at
http://www.taylorandfrancis.com

and the CRC Press Web site at
http://www.crcpress.com

This book is dedicated to my kids in fur suits.

Sherlock

Mollie

Abbey

Luna and Jagger

Contents

Preface

The objective of this book is to provide an overview of the protection of the maritime community and the methods that can be utilized to safeguard people, watercraft, ships, ports, and marinas from numerous threats. This book does not cover maritime supply chain security. The level of security varies greatly based on vessels or maritime property, and threat assessments. Because of this diversity, a wide range of security policies and a blend of physical security methods and procedures to be used in maritime security are examined.

This book is not just a presentation of facts and the reporting on how the maritime community can be protected, but also on my professional opinion and recommendations on protection methods. In the end, each vessel, marina, and port facility must make the decision as to what protective methods will be of most value.

Dr. Daniel J. Benny

Acknowledgments

My Inspiration

Sherree H. Wilson

In Appreciation

United States Navy Office of Naval Intelligence
United States Coast Guard
United States Coast Guard Auxiliary
Department of Homeland Security
Pennsylvania Fish & Boat Commission
International Association of Maritime Security Professionals

Special Thanks to

Long Level Marina owner Mindy Ritter-Hickman

In Memory of

Dick Hickman

Author

 **Dr. Daniel J. Benny** resides in Harrisburg, Pennsylvania, and is a licensed private investigator and security consultant (http:www.bennypi.com). His education and certifications include doctor of philosophy in criminal justice from Capella University, master of aeronautical science from Embry-Riddle Aeronautical University, master of arts in security administration from Norwich University, bachelor of arts in security administration from Alvernia College, associate in arts in both commercial security and police administration from Harrisburg Area Community College, and a graduate diploma from the Naval Command and Staff from the United States Naval War College. He is currently working on a master of arts in American history from Southern New Hampshire University.

Dr. Benny is board certified in security management as a Certified Protection Professional (CPP) and as a Professional Certified Investigator (PCI) in ASIS International; a Certified Fraud Examiner (CFE) by the Association of Certified Fraud Examiners; a Certified Confidentiality Officer (CCO) by the Business Espionage Controls and Countermeasures Association; a Certified Aviation Security Professional (CASP) by the American Board for Certification in Homeland Security; a Certified Institutional Protection Manager (CIPM) by the International Foundation for Cultural Property Protection; and a Certified Member (CM), an Airport Certified Employee in Security (ACE), and an Airport Security Coordinator (ASC) by the American Association of Airport Executives. He is also a Certified Vessel Security Officer (VSO) in the U.S. Coast Guard; a Marine Safety Officer and Vessel Examiner Officer in the U.S. Coast Guard Auxiliary; he holds a Federal Aviation Administration Private Pilot Certificate; he is a Cessna C-150 aircraft owner; a Commonwealth of Pennsylvania Certified Act 235 Lethal Weapons Agent; and a Black Sash in Jeet Kune Do.

The books published by Dr. Benny include: *The Complete Guide to Physical Security* (2012), *General Aviation Security: Aircraft, Hangars, Fixed-Base Operations, Flight Schools and Airports* (2012), *Cultural Property Security: Protecting Museums, Historic Sites, Archives, and Libraries* (2012), *and Industrial Espionage: Developing a Counterespionage Program* (2013), all published by CRC Press. He has also authored more than 300 articles on security matters.

Dr. Benny has served as a U.S. Naval Intelligence Officer for the Office of Naval Intelligence, the Naval Investigative Service, the Fleet Rapid Support Team, and the U.S. Central Intelligence Agency. He has also served as a U.S. Navy Police Chief.

He is a member of the following organizations: the American Society for Industrial Security International, the Association of Certified Fraud Examiners, the World Association of Detectives, the National Council of Investigation and Security Services, the Association of British Investigators, the Pennsylvania Association of Private Investigators, the Pennsylvania Association of Licensed Investigators, the American Board for Certification in Homeland Security, the International Association for Counterterrorism and Security Professionals, the International Association of Maritime Security Professionals, the International Foundation for Cultural Property Protection, the Pennsylvania Chiefs of Police Association, the National Criminal Justice Honor Society, the Association of Former Intelligence Officers, the International Spy Museum, the Business Espionage Controls & Countermeasures Association, the Naval Intelligence Professionals, the U.S. Naval War College Foundation, the U.S. Navy Memorial Foundation, the Navy League of the United States, the U.S. Naval Institute, the Military Order of the World Wars, the American Legion, the U.S. Coast Guard Auxiliary, the Boat Owners Association of the United States, the Boston Whalers Owners Club, the Council of American Maritime Museums, the Erie Maritime Museum and the Flagship Niagara League, the Jaguar Enthusiasts' Club, the MG Car Club, the Land Rover Discovery Owners Club, the Antique Automobile Club of America, the Antique Automobile Club of America Museum, the U.S. Concealed Carry Association, the National Rifle Association of America, the Harrisburg Hunters and Anglers Association, the Sherlock Holmes Society of London, the Inspector Morse Society, the Aircraft Owners and Pilots Association, American Association of Airport Association of Executives, the Aviation Council of Pennsylvania, the Air Force Association, the Civil Air Patrol, the Smithsonian Institute National Air and Space Museum Society, Ye Anciente & Secret Order of Quiet Birdmen, the Free & Accepted Masons Brownstone Lodge 666 Hershey *Master Mason*, the Ancient Accepted Scottish Rite of Freemasonry *32nd Degree*, the Academy of

Masonic Knowledge *Master Masonic Scholar*, the Pennsylvania Lodge of Research, the National Sojourners *Heroes of 76*, the Perserverance Royal Arch Chapter No. 21 of Pennsylvania, the Harrisburg Council No. 7 Royal and Select Master Masons, and the Pilgrim Commandery No. 11 Knights Templar.

Introduction

With the majority of the surface of the globe being water, most of the cargo that is shipped to, or from, the United States as well as other countries is accomplished by the maritime community, which is the economic lifeline of the country. The security of the maritime industry is vital to its continued operation and national security, which is the reason for writing this book.

The threat to the maritime community and the United States from natural threats, traditional criminal activity, piracy, and terrorism has continued from colonial days to the present. These threats have included the theft of cargo and vessels and the smuggling of people, weapons, drugs, and other contraband. During periods of war, the threats have included sabotage and espionage, such as the bombing of the Black Tom Island port and military supply depot, which was located across the water from New York City, by German saboteurs during World War I. The fight against piracy has been nonstop since the formation of the U.S. Navy to counter the Islamic pirates off the Barbary Coast to the use of the U.S. Navy Seals to free Captain Phillips during the piracy of his ship and his hijacking ordeal.

The goal of this book is to provide valuable information to assist in the development of an effective maritime security program. It is not the intent of this book to address the security of cargo in the maritime supply chain but rather to focus on the protection of ships, watercraft, and the maritime infrastructure. With the protection of the maritime industry, in turn, cargo will also be secured.

Chapters 1 and 2 explore what comprises the maritime community, such as marinas and ports. Numerous types of watercraft and ships are identified as well as the various threats to the maritime community. This includes natural threats such as storms as well as traditional criminal activity and piracy. The current terrorism threat is presented in great detail. The new threat from cyberterrorism and cybercrime is addressed in Chapter 3.

The components of a physical security program and an effective security force are examined in Chapters 4 and 5. This lays the foundation for the use of physical measures and a security force in the chapters that follow, which will cover specific areas of the maritime community.

As the book progresses to Chapters 6 through 9, the specialized areas of maritime security are addressed. This includes marine security, port security, and the protection of small watercraft, yachts, and ships.

The final chapter is an introduction to the successful U.S. Coast Guard America's Waterway Watch program. The various components of America's Waterway Watch are discussed as well as the implementation of the program at marinas, ports, and onboard watercraft and ships.

The security concepts and procedures addressed in this book will be of value to all members of the maritime community from the local boater and marina to those responsible for the protection of major ports and seagoing vessels.

CHAPTER 1

Maritime Community

The maritime community comprises many entities to include marinas, ports, and watercraft. The watercraft include small pleasure craft, yachts, and commercial and military ships.

The maritime domain serves as a critical waterway highway for the global economy. This environment presents unique security challenges encompassing vast oceans, coastal and inland waterways, commercial shipping lanes, and countless ports of entry. According to the U.S. Department of Homeland Security, the United States has 95,000 miles of coastline, 361 ports, including 8 of the world's 50 highest-volume ports and 10,000 miles of navigable waterways.

The United States has the world's largest exclusive economic zone covering 3.4 million square miles of water. This area contains some of the most productive and valuable natural resources on the globe. The Department of Homeland Security estimates that 30% of all U.S. oil supplies and 25% of all natural gas supplies are being produced in offshore areas.

According to the U.S. Coast Guard, 700 ships arrive in U.S. ports daily and 8,000 foreign-flag ships manned by 200,000 foreign mariners enter U.S. ports each year. In addition to commercial shipping, there are millions of recreational boaters who use the waterways and ports. The recreational boating industry in the United States exceeds $38 billion annually.

MARINAS

Marinas are waterfront facilities such as a dock or a port with moorings and often provide supplies to facilitate small watercraft and yachts. Marinas can be located on the coast, on intracoastal waterways, and on rivers, canals, and lakes (see Figure 1.1). An identifiable feature of a marina is that they are not used for commercial shipping and operations.

FIGURE 1.1 Docking area on a canal near Glasgow, Scotland. (Photograph by Daniel J. Benny.)

Marinas allow small pleasure watercraft and yachts the ability to be moored at docks or on mooring buoys (see Figures 1.2 and 1.3). Ramps are also provided to launch small watercraft from trailers, and designated areas for the trailers are provided close by on the shore (see Figure 1.4).

Based on the size and capabilities of the marina, various services may be offered to the maritime community. These services may include fueling, repair and sale of boats and engines, a boat supply shop, food service, pubs, restrooms, electrical power to watercraft, and watercraft waste pumping stations. Some marinas also provide clubhouse amenities such as showers, locker areas, and meeting and training rooms.

PORTS AND PORT FACILITIES

A port and port facility is a site located on a coastal waterway, a river, or a lake, which has a harbor, dock, and associated operational facilities such as administration, work, or storage buildings. The port and port facility provide one or more harbors where ships can dock and transfer people or cargo to, or from, land. The port facility may vary widely and can extend for miles. Such ports and port facilities can have an enormous positive impact on the local economy, the national transportation system, as well as national security and defense.

FIGURE 1.2　Docks at Tri-County Boat Club, Middletown, Pennsylvania. (Photograph by Daniel J. Benny.)

FIGURE 1.3　Sailboat secured to a mooring buoy at Long Level Marina in Wrightsville, Pennsylvania. (Photograph by Daniel J. Benny.)

FIGURE 1.4 The author's Boston Whaler in the trailer storage area at Long Level Marina, Wrightsville, Pennsylvania. (Photograph by Daniel J. Benny.)

Port and port facilities are selected based on location in order to optimize access to navigable water and land transportation, such as trucking, rail, and aviation for commercial operations, as well as military shipping. A port also provides shelter from wind and waves for all vessels seeking safe harbor. The type of shipping a port and port facility can handle depends on the depth of the water. Deep water ports can handle larger, more economical, and military ships (see Figure 1.5).

There are different types of ports based on the use and type of shipping and operations that occur. Ports located on coastal waters, coastal ports or inland rivers and lakes, and inland ports that can be navigated by ships can be used for cruise ships, fishing, cargo, and military operations (see Figures 1.6 through 1.9).

Some ports are used for the placement of historic ships and museums as national landmarks and for tourism (see Figure 1.10).

SMALL WATERCRAFT

Small watercraft come in a wide range of sizes and a variety of types and models based on the specific needs of the boater. Small watercraft are equipped with various types of propulsion. The most common is the outboard motor, which is attached to the transom of the watercraft with

FIGURE 1.5   The Port of Edinburgh, Scotland. (Photograph by Daniel J. Benny.)

FIGURE 1.6   Inland Port Albert Dock on the Mersey River, Liverpool, England. (Photograph by Daniel J. Benny.)

FIGURE 1.7 Fishing docks at the Port of San Diego, California. (Photograph by Daniel J. Benny.)

FIGURE 1.8 Fishing docks at the Port of San Francisco, California. (Photograph by Daniel J. Benny.)

FIGURE 1.9   Lobster boats in Rockport, Maine. (Photograph by Daniel J. Benny.)

FIGURE 1.10   The historic *USS Constellation* at the Baltimore Inner Harbor, Maryland. (Photograph by Daniel J. Benny.)

the lower unit and propeller in the water. As the lower unit turns by the use of a hand tiller or steering wheel, it turns the watercraft and moves through the water by the force of the propeller in the water. An inboard outboard is an engine that is inserted into the hull of the watercraft with a lower unit and propeller extending into the water, which operates as an outboard motor. The inboard motor is inserted into the hull of the watercraft with a shaft and propeller extending through the bottom of the hull into the water. The motor turns the propeller to move the watercraft and a rudder behind the propeller allows the watercraft to be turned (see Figure 1.11).

A jet engine is one that has an intake for the water to enter the motor and then to expel it out behind the watercraft using the force of the water to move the watercraft. A jet motor can be an outboard, inboard outboard, or an inboard, and is steered in the same manner.

Small watercraft have two basic hull designs: a displacement and planing hull. The displacement hull is designed to ride low in the water and move or displace the water as the watercraft moves through the water. This includes sailboats, kayaks, canoes, cruisers, pontoons, houseboats, tour boats, and small cabin cruisers (see Figures 1.12 through 1.15).

FIGURE 1.11   Outboard engine, Harrisburg, Pennsylvania. (Photograph by Daniel J. Benny.)

FIGURE 1.12   Sailboats in the marina at Conwy, Wales. (Photograph by Daniel J. Benny.)

FIGURE 1.13 Kayaks and a canoe on the Susquehanna River, Wrightsville, Pennsylvania. (Photograph by Daniel J. Benny.)

FIGURE 1.14   Houseboat on the Susquehanna River, Wrightsville, Pennsylvania. (Photograph by Daniel J. Benny.)

FIGURE 1.15   Cabin cruiser docking at Loch Ness, Scotland. (Photograph by Daniel J. Benny.)

FIGURE 1.16   The author's Boston Whaler at the Coast Guard Auxiliary Facility on the Susquehanna River at Long Level Marina, Wrightsville, Pennsylvania. (Photograph by Daniel J. Benny.)

The planing hull allows the watercraft to ride on top of the water once it reaches what is called planing speed. This includes runabouts, small utility boats, personal watercraft, and inflatables (see Figures 1.16 through 1.18).

The most common hulls for small watercraft are made of fiberglass and alumina (see Figures 1.19 and 1.20).

Older classic boats may be constructed of wood. Inflatable watercraft are used for sports activities, dinghies are used on larger watercraft for rescues and by law enforcement and military special operations units such as the U.S. Navy Seals. Small watercraft are also used by law enforcement operating on the waterways such as police departments located at a large port, law enforcement agencies on state waterways, and the U.S. Coast Guard (see Figures 1.21 through 1.23).

YACHTS

A yacht is a watercraft used solely for recreational enjoyment by its owner. A boat becomes a yacht at about 34 feet in length and may be up to hundreds of feet in length. A yacht can be a power-driven vessel or it

FIGURE 1.17 Utility boats at Long Level Marina, Wrightsville, Pennsylvania. (Photograph by Daniel J. Benny.)

FIGURE 1.18 Utility working boat of the National Aquarium at Baltimore Inner Harbor, Maryland. (Photograph by Daniel J. Benny.)

FIGURE 1.19 Pennsylvania Fish and Boat Commission fiberglass patrol watercraft, Harrisburg, Pennsylvania. (Photograph by Daniel J. Benny.)

FIGURE 1.20 U.S. Coast Guard Auxiliary aluminum patrol watercraft on the Susquehanna River, Middletown, Pennsylvania. (Photograph by Daniel J. Benny.)

FIGURE 1.21   Pennsylvania Fish and Boat Commission Law Enforcement patrol boat on the Susquehanna River in Middletown, Pennsylvania. (Photograph by Daniel J. Benny.)

FIGURE 1.22   Metropolitan Police of London patrol watercraft on the Thames River, London, England. (Photograph by Daniel J. Benny.)

may be powered by sails. Older yachts were constructed of wood or steel hulls. In most new construction, the hull is made of fiberglass.

Yachts can be classified as a day cruiser yacht, weekend yacht, cruising yacht, a sports fishing yacht, or a luxury yacht. The day cruiser yacht has no cabin and sparse amenities. The weekend yacht has one or two

FIGURE 1.23   Pennsylvania Fish and Boat Commission and U.S. Coast Guard patrol boats on Lake Erie, Erie, Pennsylvania. (Photograph by Daniel J. Benny.)

cabins, a galley, and a head. The cruising yacht has sufficient space and amenities to allow for living aboard for an extended period of time. The fishing yacht has quality living amenities but is equipped for extended sports fishing. The luxury yacht is similar to the cruising yacht but in most cases is larger and has more luxurious finishing and amenities (see Figure 1.24). Such yachts are prime targets for piracy because of the value of the vessel, equipment, and other items that may be onboard.

SHIPS

Cruise and Passenger Ships

A cruise ship is a vessel that is used for a maritime vacation or holiday business. The purpose is to provide a shipboard platform for the enjoyment of the passengers. Ports of call are most often included but they are not the final destination but rather are built into the vacation package of the cruise (see Figure 1.25).

Passenger ships are used to carry passengers from one point to another most often as a final destination. While some passengers may select this type of transportation because they enjoy the maritime environment, the primary role is that of a passenger service not as an entertainment holiday cruise (see Figure 1.26).

FIGURE 1.24   A luxury yacht docked at the Baltimore Inner Harbor, Maryland. (Photograph by Daniel J. Benny.)

FIGURE 1.25   Cruise ship on Loch Ness in Scotland. (Photograph by Daniel J. Benny.)

FIGURE 1.26   Passenger vessels on the Thames River, London, England. (Photograph by Daniel J. Benny.)

Cruise and passenger ships can carry a wide range of passengers and crew based on the size and gross tonnage of the ship. The ship with a weight of 4,500 gross tons can carry over 700 passengers and crew. A ship with a weight of 59,914 gross tons can carry over 3,000 passengers and crew.

Tanker Ships

A tanker ship is one that is utilized for commercial transportation of cargo across large bodies of water such as oceans, seas, and lakes, such as the Great Lakes between the United States and Canada. Tanker ships can be identified by the type of cargo that they carry. This includes crude oil, liquefied natural gas, and chemicals (see Figure 1.27).

Container Ships

Container ships are those that carry a variety of cargo. Unlike loading cargo as individual items as was the practice many years ago, the cargo is now first loaded into metal containers. The containers are transported to the dock facilities by truck or rail. The containers are then loaded onto the container ship.

FIGURE 1.27   Tanker ships off of Virginia Beach, Virginia. (Photograph by Daniel J. Benny.)

Oceangoing Tugboats

Tugboats are work vessels that are used in harbors to aid in the mooring, unmooring, and movement of ships. Oceangoing tugboats are much larger and more powerful than harbor tugboats. They are most often used for towing a ship in distress in open waters and for salvage operations (see Figure 1.28).

Military Ships

Military ships are vessels that are used as part of a military service. The military ships that arrive at port facilities can be from any nation that is permitted access to the nation's waters where the port is located (see Figures 1.29 and 1.30).

STATE, TERRITORY, AND LOCAL WATERWAY LAW ENFORCEMENT AGENCIES

All 50 states and territories of the United States have a state law enforcement agency responsible for the enforcement of laws related to the use of waterways in their jurisdiction (see the list of State, Territory Law Enforcement Agencies later). Some of the agencies are designated as maritime police, others as waterway conservation officers, and some are

FIGURE 1.28   A tugboat with a U.S. Navy submarine at Norfolk, Virginia. (Photograph by Daniel J. Benny.)

FIGURE 1.29   U.S. Navy ships at Norfolk, Virginia. (Photograph by Daniel J. Benny.)

FIGURE 1.30 U.S. Navy ship on the Mississippi River near New Orleans, Louisiana. (Photograph by Daniel J. Benny.)

combined with wildlife enforcement (see Figure 1.31). In some states, the state police are assigned this responsibility.

Based on the location and type of waters in the state, be it streams, rivers, lakes, bays, or the seacoast, the enforcement and type of law enforcement watercraft used will vary. One standardization is that all law enforcement watercraft will display a blue light.

FIGURE 1.31 Pennsylvania Fish and Boat Commission Headquarters, Harrisburg, Pennsylvania. (Photograph by Daniel J. Benny.)

FIGURE 1.32   Baltimore Police patrol vehicle at the Baltimore Inner Harbor, Maryland. (Photograph by Daniel J. Benny.)

Larger cities located on the water such as the Great Lakes, rivers, bays, and the seacoast may also have a waterway law enforcement division of their police department (see Figure 1.32).

For a list of all the United States and territory boating law enforcement agencies, see Appendix A.

U.S. Coast Guard

The U.S. Coast Guard is simultaneously a military force and federal law enforcement agency dedicated to safety, security, and stewardship missions. The mission of the U.S. Coast Guard is to save lives, protect the environment, defend the homeland, and to enforce federal laws on the high seas, the nation's coastal waters, and its inland waterways (see Figure 1.33).

The Coast Guard's official history began on August 4, 1790 when President George Washington signed the Tariff Act that authorized the construction of 10 vessels, referred to as "cutters," to enforce federal tariff and trade laws and to prevent smuggling. Known by various names throughout the nineteenth and early twentieth centuries such as the "revenue cutters," the "system of cutters," and finally the "Revenue Cutter Service," it expanded in size and responsibility as the nation grew.

FIGURE 1.33 U.S. Coast Guard patrol boat at Cape May, New Jersey. (Photograph by Daniel J. Benny.)

The service received its present name in 1915 under an act of Congress that merged the Revenue Cutter Service with the U.S. Life-Saving Service, thereby providing the nation with a single maritime service dedicated to saving lives at sea and enforcing the nation's maritime laws. The Coast Guard began maintaining the country's aid to maritime navigation, including lighthouses, when President Franklin Roosevelt ordered the transfer of the Lighthouse Service to the Coast Guard in 1939. In 1946, Congress permanently transferred the Commerce Department's Bureau of Marine Inspection and Navigation to the Coast Guard, thereby placing merchant marine licensing and merchant vessel safety under its purview.

The Coast Guard is one of the oldest organizations of the federal government and until Congress established the Navy Department in 1798, it served as the nation's only armed force afloat. The Coast Guard protected the nation throughout its long history and served proudly in every one of the nation's conflicts. The Coast Guard's national defense responsibilities remain one of its most important functions even today. In times of peace, it operates as part of the Department of Homeland Security, serving as the nation's frontline agency for enforcing the

FIGURE 1.34 U.S. Coast Guard *Eagle*, New London, Connecticut. (Photograph by Daniel J. Benny.)

nation's laws at sea, protecting the marine environment and the nation's vast coastline and ports, and saving lives. In times of war, or at the direction of the president, the Coast Guard serves as part of the Navy Department (Figure 1.34).

One of the U.S. Coast Guard's current missions as it relates to maritime security was established by the Homeland Security Act of 2002, which divided the Coast Guard's 11 statutory missions between homeland security and non-homeland security. Reflecting the Coast Guard's historical role in defending our nation, the Act delineated Ports, Waterways, and Coastal Security as the first homeland security mission. The Commandant of the Coast Guard designated Ports, Waterways, and Coastal Security as the service's primary focus alongside search and rescue.

The Ports, Waterways, and Coastal Security mission entails the protection of the U.S. Maritime Domain and the U.S. Marine Transportation System and those who live, work, or recreate near them; the prevention and disruption of terrorist attacks, sabotage, espionage, or subversive acts; and response to and recovery from those that do occur. Conducting Ports, Waterways, and Coastal Security deters terrorists from using or exploiting the Maritime Transportation System as a means for attacks on U.S. territory, population centers, vessels, critical infrastructure, and key resources. Ports, Waterways, and Coastal Security include the employment of awareness activities; counterterrorism, antiterrorism, preparedness and response operations; and the establishment and oversight of a maritime security regime. Ports, Waterways, and Coastal Security also include the national defense role of protecting military out load operations.

In 2003, the Coast Guard addressed its Ports, Waterways, and Coastal Security responsibilities and functions by initiating Operation Neptune Shield. The Coast Guard supplemented Operation Neptune Shield with tactical and strategic documents the *2006 Coast Guard Strategic Plan for Combating Maritime Terrorism, and the 2008 Combating Maritime Terrorism Strategic and Performance Plan.*

The Coast Guard's systematic, maritime governance model for Ports, Waterways, and Coastal Security employs a triad consisting of domain awareness, maritime security regimes, and maritime security and response operations carried out in a unified effort by international, governmental, and private stakeholders.

Maritime domain awareness means the effective understanding of anything associated with the maritime domain that could impact the security, safety, economy, or environment of the United States. Attaining and sustaining an effective understanding and awareness of the maritime domain require the collection, fusion, analysis, and dissemination of prioritized categories of data, information, and intelligence. These are collected during the conduct of all Coast Guard missions. Awareness input comes from Field Intelligence Support Teams, Maritime Intelligence Fusion Centers, the Nationwide Automatic Identification System, other vessel-tracking systems, and the public reporting suspicious incidents through America's Waterway Watch program.

Maritime security regimes comprise a system of rules that shape acceptable activities in the maritime domain. Regimes include domestic and international protocols and/or frameworks that coordinate partnerships, establish maritime security standards, collectively engage in shared maritime security interests, and facilitate the sharing of information. Domestically, the Coast Guard–led Area Maritime Security Committees carry out much of the maritime security regimes effort. Abroad, the Coast Guard works with individual countries and through the International Maritime Organization, a specialized agency of the United Nations. Together, regimes and domain awareness inform decision makers and allow them to identify trends, anomalies, and activities that threaten or endanger U.S. interests.

Defeating terrorism requires integrated, comprehensive operations that maximize effectiveness without duplicating efforts. Security and response operations consist of counterterrorism and antiterrorism activities. Counterterrorism activities are offensive in nature. The Maritime Security Response Team is a highly specialized resource with advanced counterterrorism skills and tactics. The Maritime Security Response Team is trained to be a first responder to potential terrorist situations; deny terrorist acts; perform security actions against noncompliant actors; perform tactical facility entry and enforcement; participate in port-level counterterrorism exercises; and educate other forces on Coast Guard counterterrorism procedures.

Antiterrorism activities are defensive in nature. As a maritime security agency, the Coast Guard uses its unique authorities, competencies, capacities, operational capabilities and partnerships to board suspect vessels, escort ships deemed to present or be at significant risk, enforce fixed security zones at maritime critical infrastructure and key resources, and patrol the maritime approaches, coasts, ports, and rivers of America. Coast Guard cutters, boats, helicopters, and shoreside patrols are appropriately armed and trained. Many current and planned antiterrorism activities support the Department of Homeland Security Small Vessel Security Strategy. Twelve Maritime Safety and Security Teams enforce security zones, conduct port–state control boardings, protect military out-load vessels, ensure maritime security during major marine events, augment shoreside security at waterfront facilities, detect weapons of mass destruction, and participate in port-level antiterrorism exercises in their home ports and other ports to which elements of the 12 Maritime Safety and Security Teams may be assigned for operations (see Figure 1.35).

Viewing maritime initiatives and policies as part of a larger system enables a better understanding of their relationships and effectiveness. A well-designed system of regimes, awareness, and operational capabilities creates overlapping domestic and international safety nets, layers of security, and effective stewardship making it that much harder for terrorists to succeed.

U.S. Coast Guard Auxiliary

Boating has always been one of America's favorite pastimes and entered the sports arena in the early nineteenth century. Rowing and yachting races were among the most popular spectator sports through the 1930s. The wealth generated in post–Civil War America, along with the growth of railroads, spurred the development of resorts, country homes, and suburbs—all places to go boating. The federal government began to construct large dams, reservoirs, and lake systems during the Depression, adding to waterways. With the development of the single-operator motorboat and the outboard engine at the turn of the twentieth

FIGURE 1.35   U.S. Coast Guard helicopter used for maritime patrol at Cape May, New Jersey. (Photograph by Daniel J. Benny.)

century, the number of recreational boaters skyrocketed. In 1939, the Coast Guard reported that there were more than 300,000 boats operating in federal waters. In the previous year, it had received 14,000 calls for assistance and had responded to 8,600 "in peril" cases—a record number. Boaters needed to be better trained in seamanship and federal law. At the same time, civilian yachtsmen were pressing the Coast Guard to establish a volunteer arm of the service.

As a result of these demands, on June 23, 1939, the Congress passed legislation that established the Coast Guard Reserve, its volunteer civilian component, to promote boating safety and to facilitate the operations of the Coast Guard. Groups of boat owners were organized into flotillas and these into divisions within Coast Guard districts around the country. Members initially conducted safety and security patrols and helped enforce the provisions of the 1940 Federal Boating and Espionage Acts. Then in February 1941, a military reserve was created and the Volunteer Reserve was renamed the U.S. Coast Guard Auxiliary.

Following America's entry into World War II in December of 1941, recruits flooded into Auxiliary flotillas in a burst of patriotic fervor. June 1942 legislation allowed Auxiliarists to enroll in the Coast Guard Reserve on a part-time temporary basis. Throughout the war, some 50,000 Auxiliarists constituted the core of the temporary Reserve membership. These reservists, along with newly enrolled civilians, performed coastal defense and search and rescue duties. They patrolled bridges, factories, docks, and beaches. They fought fires, made arrests, guided Naval vessels, and conducted antisubmarine warfare. As their ranks grew, thousands of active duty Coast Guard personnel were freed up for service overseas.

Following the war, by 1950 the four traditional Auxiliary cornerstone missions of public education, operations, vessel examination, and fellowship had been established. The public education program yearly trains tens of thousands of boaters in seamanship, piloting, rules of the water, and weather, among other topics. Specially qualified coxswain and crew members conduct search and rescue missions on their own boats and support Coast Guard missions. Auxiliary pilots and air observers search for boaters in distress, floating hazards, pollution spills, and ice-locked vessels (see Figure 1.36). Communications watchstanders handle distress calls at Coast Guard and Auxiliary radio stations. Vessel examiners conduct Vessel Safety Checks under which recreational vessels are examined for properly installed federally required equipment and systems.

During the past decades, the Auxiliary has continued to grow in membership which today totals more than 30,000 members in the United States and its territories. Training is held at every level from the flotilla to national training schools. Leadership and management training, award programs, and data management systems ensure a high level of professionalism.

FIGURE 1.36 U.S. Coast Guard Auxiliary safety patrol on the Susquehanna River in Middletown, Pennsylvania. (Photograph by Daniel J. Benny.)

Under legislation passed in 1996, the Auxiliary's role was expanded to allow members to assist in any Coast Guard mission, except direct law enforcement and military operations, as authorized by the Commandant. The U.S. Coast Guard Auxiliary members can be found examining commercial fishing vessels, flying in C-130 aircraft, working in Coast Guard offices, and crewing with regulars. The three components of the service—the active duty Coastguardsmen, the Reservists, and Auxiliarists truly constitute team Coast Guard.

Auxiliary members work an untold number of hours, as they largely administer their own organization. Since 9/11, members have been integrated into the Department of Homeland Security and perform a variety of port security functions. Over the years, Auxiliary programs also have kept pace with boating trends. Members helped implement the provisions of the 1958 Federal Boating Act. In the 1970s, they formed flotillas in sole-state waters to meet local demands for water safety. They introduced new courses such as those for sailors and personal watercraft (PWC) operators as their numbers increased.

The U.S. Coast Guard Auxiliary is the largest volunteer marine safety organization in the world and has fostered similar ones in foreign countries. The U.S. Coast Guard Auxiliary's current primary missions include support for the U.S. Coast Guard, homeland security, marine safety programs; watercraft safety, search and rescue patrols; public boating safety education; and vessel safety checks. During its 60 years, it has lived up to its motto of—"A Proud Tradition, A Worthy Mission."

U.S. Power Squadron

The U.S. Power Squadron was organized in 1914 as a nonprofit, educational organization dedicated to boating safety through education in seamanship, navigation, and related subjects. It was also established to participate with our fellow members on the water and in the classroom. The U.S. Power Squadron has nearly 40,000 members organized into over 400 squadrons across the country and in some U.S. territories. Each squadron's activities involve the three primary objectives of the U.S. Power Squadron: community service, continuing education, and enjoying the friendship and camaraderie of our fellow members.

Local squadrons offer boating safety courses on a regular basis to boaters in our communities. These courses are open to the public and there is no age limit for participants. Successfully completing the U.S. Power Squadron boating safety course meets the educational requirements for boat operation in all states.

In a cooperative program with the U.S. Coast Guard Auxiliary, squadron members conduct courtesy Vessel Safety Checks of boats at the request of their owners. The members also help the National Ocean Service maintain the accuracy of U.S. nautical charts by reporting chart corrections; and local squadrons participate in many other community improvement projects.

Every squadron offers many carefully planned courses in subjects like Seamanship, Piloting, Plotting and Position Finding, Celestial Navigation, Cruise Planning, Engine Maintenance, Marine Electronics, Sailing, and much more. These courses are taught by experienced member instructors.

Participating both on-the-water and off with fellow members who are skilled in boating is a rewarding and enjoyable experience. On-the-water activities include cruises, rendezvous, sailing races, navigation contests, and even fishing derbies. Activities ashore include meetings with marine programs, parties, dinner dances, picnics, and field trips.

Boat Owners Association of the United States

The Boat Owners Association of the United States has worked to provide quality service, savings, and representation to the boating community since it was founded in 1966. At present, the Boat Owners Association of the United States has over half a million members.

The Boat Owners Association of the United States provides it members' savings on over 1,000 boating businesses for discounts on fuel, transient slips, repairs, insurance, and more. It also offers on-the-water and on-the-road towing service levels provided by the nation's largest towing fleet and insures billions of dollars' worth of members' boats offering unparalleled service at competitive prices.

The members of the Boat Owners Association of the United States also obtain valuable information for the organization's monthly publication and website. Information on the website covers safety and security issues of importance to boaters, boat owners, and marinas.

International Association of Maritime Security Professionals

The mission of the International Association of Maritime Security Professionals is to serve as the preeminent association of security professionals operating within the maritime environment. This has been achieved through the development of maritime security standards, guidelines, and practices. The development of maritime security education programs provides a community of trusted professionals that can work collaboratively in the maritime security profession.

The International Association of Maritime Security Professionals established the Certified Maritime Security Professional (CMSP) designation for those working specifically in the maritime security profession. To earn the designation, the candidate must have positive references, 5 years of experience in maritime security, pass a certification exam, and agree to follow the code of values and ethics of the International Association of Maritime Security Professionals.

> **MARITIME SECURITY PROFESSIONALS: VOLUNTARY PROFESSIONAL CODE OF PRACTICE**

1.0 INTRODUCTION

The International Association of Maritime Security Professionals (IAMSP) was created after a number of maritime security companies identified that there was a clear need for self-regulation within the maritime security industry. The organization's aim is to set high standards of best practice within the industry and form a body capable of offering authoritative advice to maritime security practitioners and related research to the wider maritime community. The term *MarSecPro* is also used as an informal reference to *Maritime Security Professionals*.

This Voluntary Code sets out the professional standards required by the IAMSP, also known as "MarSecPro," as a condition of holding membership with the organization. It applies to Maritime Security Professionals at all membership grades. Within this document, the term "relevant authority" is used to identify the person or organization which has authority over your activity as an individual. If you are a practicing Maritime Security Professional, this is normally a private security company that you may be subcontracted to or the client. The Code governs your personal conduct as a Maritime Security Professional and not the nature of business or ethics of the relevant authority. It will, therefore, be a matter of you exercising your personal judgment in meeting the requirements of this Code.

2.0 THE MarSecPro STANDARD

The overarching aim and objectives of IAMSP are to maintain and promote high standards of ethical practice in the provision of maritime protective security services; this is referred to as the "MarSecPro standard":

> 2.1 Establish and promote high-quality education and personal development at all levels throughout the Maritime Security Professional's career in the maritime security industry

2.2 To define the professional standards expected of Maritime Security Professionals

2.3 To provide an internationally recognized Certification scheme for Maritime Security Professionals

2.4 To initiate, develop, evaluate, and communicate Maritime Security, standards, and good practices

2.5 To influence client managers, policy makers, and other stakeholders worldwide in Maritime Security issues

3.0 THE PUBLIC INTEREST

3.1 *Health and Safety*: At all times in your professional role you shall have regard for public health, safety, and the environment.

    3.1.1 This is a general responsibility, which may be governed by legislation, convention, or protocol.

    3.1.2 If in doubt over the appropriate course of action to take in particular circumstances, you should seek the advice of a peer or colleague.

3.2 *Third Parties*: You shall have regard to the legitimate rights of third parties.

    3.2.1 The term "Third Party" includes professional colleagues, or possibly competitors, or members of "the public" who might be affected by your work as a Maritime Security Professional without their direct awareness of the existence of your work.

3.3 *Legal*: Maritime Security Professionals should undertake at all times to comply with or observe all applicable laws and regulations, wherever they operate.

    3.3.1 Maritime Security Professionals, whether acting for themselves or an employer, should not take any action that they know, or reasonably should know, would violate any applicable law or regulation.

    3.3.2 Maritime Security Professionals must ensure that their conduct cannot be interpreted as breaching the laws; if unsure, they must consult, at the earliest possible stage of business dealings, with a suitably qualified and knowledgeable person.

    3.3.3 Maritime Security Professionals should take into account the culture of the maritime assets flag state, crew, or the country or region in which they are operating.

3.4 *Discrimination*: You shall conduct your professional activities without discrimination against clients, colleagues, or fellow members of the maritime security industry.

    3.4.1 Grounds of discrimination include, but are not limited to race, color, ethnic origin, gender, sexual orientation, age, and disability.

3.4.2 All colleagues have a right to be treated with dignity and respect.

3.4.3 You should adhere to the relevant law within the jurisdiction where you are working.

3.5 *Bribery*: Maritime Security Professionals shall not accept nor make any offer of bribery or inducement.

4.0 DUTY TO RELEVANT AUTHORITY

4.1 *Challenges to Your Judgment*: You shall carry out work with due care and diligence in accordance with the relevant authority's requirements. If your professional judgment is overruled, you shall indicate the likely risks and consequences given in the following.

4.1.1 Be aware of the potential conflict between full and committed compliance with the "relevant authority's" wishes, and the independent and considered exercise of your judgment.

4.1.2 If your judgment is overruled, you are encouraged to seek advice and guidance from a peer or colleague on how best to respond.

4.2 *Conflict of Interest*: You shall avoid any situation that may give rise to a conflict of interest between you and your relevant authority. You shall make full and immediate disclosure to them if any conflict is likely to occur or be seen by a third party as likely to occur.

4.3 *Confidentiality*: Maritime Security Professionals must respect privacy and confidentiality of information and understand that they are privileged to access certain information as a result of their professional activities. You shall not disclose or authorize to be disclosed, or use for personal gain or to benefit a third party, confidential information except with the permission of your relevant authority, or at the direction of a court of law.

4.4 *Use of Information*: You shall not misrepresent or withhold information on the findings of security reports, performance of systems or services, or take advantage of the lack of relevant knowledge or inexperience of others.

4.5 *Competition*: Maritime Security Professionals might, from time to time, provide services to relevant authorities who may be in competition with each other or who offer similar products or services. If this is the case, Maritime Security Professionals must declare any potential conflict of interest which might arise.

4.6 *Delivery of Services*: Maritime Security Professionals shall strive to deliver the most cost-effective solutions consistent with the needs of the relevant authority.

5.0 DUTY TO THE PROFESSION AND MARSECPRO (THE INTERNATIONAL ASSOCIATION OF MARITIME SECURITY PROFESSIONALS)

5.1 *Reputation*: You shall uphold the reputation and good standing of the MarSecPro standard in particular, and the maritime security profession in general, and shall seek to improve professional standards through the MarSecPro Code of Practice and through participation in their development, use, and enforcement.

    5.1.1 As a Maritime Security Professional you also have a wider responsibility to promote good practice and, whenever practical, to counter misinformation that brings or could bring the profession into disrepute.

    5.1.2 You should encourage and support fellow Maritime Security Professionals in their professional development.

5.2 *Integrity*: You shall act with integrity in your relationships with all Maritime Security Professionals and with members of other professions with whom you work in a professional capacity.

5.3 *Representation*: You shall have due regard for the possible consequences of your statements on others. You shall not make any public statement in your professional capacity unless you are properly qualified and, where appropriate, authorized to do so. You shall not claim to represent MarSecPro unless authorized to do so. For the elimination of doubt, this would normally only be Directors and Officials of the International Association of Maritime Security Professionals, unless otherwise specifically invited to do so.

    5.3.1 The offering of an opinion in public, holding oneself out to be an expert in the subject in question, is a major personal responsibility and should not be undertaken lightly.

    5.3.2 To give an opinion that subsequently proves ill founded is a disservice to the profession and to MarSecPro.

5.4 *Conduct*: Maritime Security Professionals should not conduct themselves in a manner which is seriously prejudicial to MarSecPro and should not officially represent any organization whose aims and objectives are damaging to MarSecPro.

5.5 *Notification*: You are required to notify MarSecPro if convicted of a criminal offence or upon becoming bankrupt or disqualified as a Company Director. Not all convictions are seen as relevant to holding MarSecPro membership and each case will be considered individually.

6.0 PROFESSIONAL COMPETENCE AND INTEGRITY

6.1 *Career Professional Development*: You shall seek to upgrade your professional knowledge and skill and shall maintain awareness of technological developments, procedures, and standards which are relevant to your field and encourage your subordinates to do likewise.

6.2 *Scope of Competence*: You shall not claim any level of competence that you do not possess. You shall only offer to do work or provide a service that is within your professional competence.

6.3 *Self-Assessment*: You can self-assess your professional competence for undertaking a particular job or role by asking, for example:

6.3.1 Am I familiar with the service involved, or have I delivered similar services earlier?

6.3.2 Have I successfully completed similar assignments or roles in the past?

6.3.3 Can I demonstrate adequate knowledge of the specific job requirements to successfully undertake the work?

6.4 *Responsibility*: You shall accept professional responsibility for your work and for the work of colleagues who you may be responsible for and are under your direction.

INTERNATIONAL MARITIME ORGANIZATION: INTERNATIONAL SHIP AND PORT FACILITY SECURITY CODE

After the events of September 11, 2001, a Diplomatic Conference on maritime security was held at the Headquarters of the International Maritime Organization in London, England. An amendment to the 1974 International Convention for the Safety of Life at Sea was adopted. This amendment was called the International Ship and Port Facility Security Code ISPS Code (see Figure 1.37).

This International Maritime Organization ISPS Code that went into effect on July 1, 2004, requires that there are properly trained personnel for port facilities and crew for ships in order to effectively carry out their assigned security duties. These security duties include physical security of the ports and ship, access control, the restriction of unauthorized weapons and contraband, a system in place to raise alarm and to establish security communications. The International Maritime Organization's International Ship and Port Facility Security Code also requires the completion of security risk assessments, the development of security procedures, and the training and conducting of drills for personnel and crew.

FIGURE 1.37 International Maritime Organization International Ship and Port Facility Security Code. (Photograph by Daniel J. Benny.)

The goal of the International Maritime Organization ISPS Code prevents and reduces all criminal activity to include terrorism, piracy, hijacking, sabotage, smuggling of drugs and contraband, stowaways, theft, vandalism, and cargo tampering. It was also developed to prevent the use of the vessel to carry perpetrators and equipment to be used in crime or the use of the vessel as a weapon.

Specific aspects of this Code will be addressed in the relevant chapters of this text.

U.S. Coast Guard: Maritime Transportation Security Act of 2002

The Maritime Transportation Security Act of 2002 (33 CFR 101–106) that was passed and signed into law by President George W. Bush in 2002 mandates the following of the ISPS Code for U.S. flag vessels. The Maritime Transportation Security Act (33 CFR 103–104) covering vessel security and area security authorized maritime security regulations similar to the ISPS Code. The U.S. Coast Guard that now operating under the Department of Homeland Security is responsible for verifying that each affected vessel complies with the Maritime Transportation Security Act.

The Maritime Transportation Security Act covers the ship security plan, port facility security plan, the role of the ship, port and company security officer, ship alarm systems, and the shipboard automatic identification system. The maritime security of Maritime Security (MARSEC) Levels is also discussed. Details of the Maritime Transportation Security Act and how it applies to port facilities and ship security will be addressed in detail in the relevant chapters of this text.

Security and Accountability for Every Port Act of 2006

The Security and Accountability for Every Port Act was passed on May 4, 2006 and signed into law by President George W. Bush on October 13, 2006. Known as the Safe Port Act was an enhancement to the Maritime Transportation Act of 2002, in that it codified various aspects and programs of the Maritime Transportation Act of 2002. Areas that were codified included the Container Security Initiatives and the Customs–Trade Partnership Against Terrorism.

Other provisions included the requirement that all containers entering high-volume U.S. seaports be scanned for sources of radiation. It also codified the Transportation Worker Identification Credential (TWIC) to be issued for access and work at U.S. seaport facilities.

Office of Naval Intelligence: National Maritime Intelligence Center

America is a maritime nation whose security and prosperity depend on the free navigation of the world's oceans. The Office of Naval Intelligence services is dedicated on ensuring the security of the United States homeland and freedom of the seas by enabling information dominance for national and naval leaders. Our activities are guided by the objectives given in the following:

- Prevent criminal or hostile acts against the United States and its people
- Protect maritime-related population centers and critical infrastructures
- Minimize damage and expedite recovery from attack
- Safeguard the ocean and its resources

FIGURE 1.38 The author LT. Daniel J. Benny in 1993 when assigned to the Office of Naval Intelligence, the National Maritime Intelligence Center in Suitland, Maryland. (Official U.S. Navy photograph.)

Established in 1882, the Office of Naval Intelligence is America's longest continuously operating intelligence service. We employ world-class analysts, engineers, technicians, leaders, and managers. Consequently, the Office of Naval Intelligence maintains a position of unparalleled leadership in the collection, analysis, and production of scientific, technical, geopolitical, military, and maritime intelligence. The Office of Naval Intelligence employs more than 3,000 military and civilian intelligence professionals including active and reserve officers and enlisted sailors and marines and contracted personnel at the modern National Maritime Intelligence Center facility in Washington, DC, and at other strategic locations around the world (see Figure 1.38).

On October 20, 1993, the Office of Naval Intelligence dedicated its new headquarters and the National Maritime Intelligence Center in Suitland, Maryland. This joint maritime intelligence center has the mission of providing specialized maritime intelligence analysis and operates in an oversight capacity with regard to security and intelligence issues for the U.S. Navy. It also works closely with U.S. Coast Guard Intelligence in providing security for U.S. waterways, ports, and port facilities.

BIBLIOGRAPHY

International Maritime Organization. (2012). *Guide to maritime security and the ISPS code*. London, UK: International Maritime Organization.

Mid-Atlantic Maritime Academy. (2012). *Vessel security officer*. Virginia Beach, VA: Mid-Atlantic Maritime Academy.

United States Coast Guard. (2002). *Maritime strategy for homeland security*. Washington, DC: U.S. Government Printing Office.

United States Coast Guard. (2014). *United States counter piracy and maritime security action plan*. Washington, DC: U.S. Government Printing Office.

United States Department of Homeland Security. (2008). *Small vessel security strategy*. Washington, DC: U.S. Government Printing Office.

United States Power Squadron/University of West Florida. (2012). *USPS University/University of West Florida Seminar Small Boat Security*. Pensacola, FL: University of West Florida.

CHAPTER 2

Security Threats to the Maritime Community

The threat to the maritime community, its ships, cargo, and port facilities from natural threats, traditional criminal activity, piracy, and terrorism has existed throughout seafaring history. These threats to the America maritime community have continued from colonial days to the present.

The threats have included weather, the theft of cargo and vessels, as well as the smuggling of people, weapons, drugs, and other contraband. During periods of war, the threats have included sabotage and espionage. The fight against piracy has been nonstop from the formation of the U.S. Navy to counter the pirates on the Barbary Coast to the use of the U.S. Navy Seals to free Captain Phillips during his piracy and hijacking ordeal.

In recent decades until the present, there has been the threat of terrorism to the maritime community and the homeland of the United States of America. This led to the development of the *U.S. Coast Guard Maritime Strategy for Homeland Security in 2002* in which the protection of U.S. ports and ships was reevaluated to counter the emerging threat of terrorism.

The elements of this current U.S. Coast Guard strategy include an increase in maritime domain awareness for early detection of possible terrorism and conducting enhanced maritime security operations to detect and interpret terrorist activities.

Additional measures have included increasing physical security for ports. The final aspect of the strategy is to build partnerships with the maritime community and to ensure readiness for timely and effective homeland security operations.

NATURAL THREATS

Natural threats are the consequence of natural weather activity that can have severe effects on vessels and port facilities. The natural threats that can threaten vessels may include heavy seas, high winds, lightning, extreme temperatures, fog, heavy rain, snow, or ice; and may also include unknown obstruction or smoke. Natural threats such as high winds, high seas, lightning, extreme temperatures, heavy rain, snow, and ice cannot impact port facilities (Figure 2.1).

These natural threats can also be a direct threat to individuals such as the crews on vessels or employees at port facilities. As it relates to the security of vessels and port facilities, natural threats can impact physical security by rendering security systems and barriers on vessels and onshore inactive or degraded. Such natural threats may also force vessels to seek safety from a natural threat in unknown ports, only to make them vulnerable to human security threats based on the location of the unknown port.

Natural threats cannot always be prevented but the impact can be mitigated. This can be accomplished by conducting natural threat assessments and formulating plans on how to in some cases avoid the natural threat. This includes not going on the water when a serious storm is

FIGURE 2.1 With the sea environment there are numerous natural threats to the maritime community. Sunrise at Virginia Beach, Virginia. (Photograph by Daniel J. Benny.)

forecast or to move ships from the areas before the storm arrives. When the natural threat cannot be avoided by having an effective emergency management plan, the losses due to the natural threat can be reduced and the recovery from the threat will be more effective.

Natural threats need to be identified and calculated into the impact on the security of maritime port facilities and vessels. Based on the identified natural threats, physical security and security operations need to be flexible to ensure that security is not denigrated during such events.

TRADITIONAL CRIMINAL ACTIVITY

Traditional criminal activity can target maritime buildings and structures in the form of arson and vandalism. It may also include burglary and theft of property, merchandise, or cargo stored in the buildings or the docks. The theft of valuable information stored in buildings in the form of documents or electronic data on computers is also a serious threat to the maritime community in the form of fraud, identity theft, or industrial espionage.

Similar criminal activity can target small watercraft, yachts, and commercial shipping. This includes the theft of a small watercraft, electronics, and navigation equipment on vessels. Property of value, cargo as well as information can be taken from vessels of all types and tonnage. Vandalism of watercraft is also a serious problem especially for small watercraft at marinas. This may include damage to the craft, cutting it loose from its mooring, or even sinking the watercraft by drilling holes in the hull or removing the boat's drain plug (see Figure 2.2).

Traditional criminal activity can also target individuals in the maritime community. This may be in the form of an outside threat such as murder, robbery, rape, and assault. These same crimes could be internal as a workplace violence incident involving other employees. Domestic violence could also be carried into the maritime workplace by a family member of an employee or a visitor.

Piracy and terrorism, which are covered next, are serious threats to the maritime community but the most frequent threats will be from traditional crime at shore-based facilities, ports, and on ships. Maritime cargo and vessels are progressively being targeted by organized criminals to include alien smuggling, cargo theft, and drug smuggling.

PIRACY AND TERRORISM

The United Nations Convention on the Law of the Sea, Article 101, defines piracy as the following acts: illegal acts of violence or detention

FIGURE 2.2 A small watercraft sunk as a result of vandalism. (Photograph by Daniel J. Benny.)

or any act of depredation committed for private ends by the crew or the passengers of a private vessel or private aircraft and directed on the high seas against another vessel or aircraft or against a person or property onboard such a vessel or aircraft. It also includes acts against a vessel, an aircraft, a person, or property in a place outside of the jurisdiction of any state. Most attacks on vessels occur in port. This, however, does not meet the definition of piracy. The United States has its own piracy laws (see Appendix D).

Piracy is part of maritime history—pirates threatened various trading routes of Ancient Greece, Roman ships were attacked by pirates and were seized for their cargoes of grain and olive oil. The Vikings, which means *sea raiders*, were feared for their tactics of attacking shipping and coastal settlements.

During the golden age of piracy, 1600–1800, there were privateers, buccaneers, and corsairs. Privateers were authorized by their government to attack and pillage enemy nation ships. Privateers would share their profits with the government. Buccaneers were pirates who operated from bases in the West Indies and attacked primarily Spanish shipping in the Caribbean. Other ships were also targeted. Corsairs were Muslim pirates who were active in the Mediterranean. The Barbary

Corsairs were Muslim and operated solely from the North African states of Algiers, Tunis, Tripoli, and Morocco, and were authorized by their governments to attack the ships of Christian countries. It was based on this threat to shipping in the United States that the U.S. Navy was established.

Piracy was also prevalent in the waters off of the United States. The pirate Blackbeard, Edward Teach, kidnapped prominent South Carolinians and blockaded the wealthy port city of Charleston, South Carolina. Slaves were also shipped by vessels for enormous profits by some pirates. In New Orleans, Louisiana, Jean Laffitte ran a piracy ring. His illegal activities were prosperous that his operations accounted for one-tenth of the employment in the city of New Orleans.

Piracy continues to this day. Pirates today seek money as in the past but most now are associated with terrorist groups that take part in the activity to obtain money and material support for their terror operations as well as the media attention to disseminate the views of their cause.

To understand and counter the threat from terrorism, it is important to have a grasp of the strategies and tactics employed by terrorist organizations. It is also important to understand why they are such a threat. You may have heard the words, "One man's terrorist is another man's freedom fighter." It may be hard to agree on what a freedom fighter is, but a group of individuals who specifically target civilians are not freedom fighters, they are terrorists. A good terrorist is a dead terrorist.

There are many different definitions of terrorism. The most direct definition is as follows: the use or threat of violence to obtain specific goals. There are four basic goals of terrorist organizations. Depending on the terrorist group, it may be one of the following goals or a combination of several of them.

Political Goals

The political goal is to change the leadership or political structure of a country. An example of this would be the conflict between the United Kingdom and Ireland over the control of Northern Ireland. While often both sides had different religious affiliations, the real issue was political.

Ideological Goals

This includes terrorist groups whose goal is to stop a certain practice. This may include animal rights, environmental, or antiabortion groups who take part in criminal acts in support of their ideological cause.

Religious Goals

Some terrorist organizations base their action on religious views such as Islamic Jihadists. Their goal is to convert the earth to Islam by force if necessary. Islamic Jihadists goals are also political and ideological because Islam is a way of life and is their political and judicial system.

Violence for Effect

The ultimate goals are to influence an audience beyond the immediate victim(s). They want to attract attention to the cause, demonstrate power, exact revenge, obtain logistical support to carry out terrorist operations, and if possible cause government overreaction to gain support of the masses and media.

Terrorist Categories

There are three specific categories of terrorists: state directed, state supported, and non-state supported. State directed is when a county uses terrorism as a matter of their national policy such as Iran. State supported is when a country provides aid to terrorism in the form of money, weapons, or harboring terrorists in their country as was the case in Iraq. Non-state supported terrorists are terrorist groups who operate independently with no assistance from a nation. This includes domestic groups such as the Klu Klux Klan or Black Panthers.

There are two broad categories of terrorist organizations, the national terrorist and the transnational terrorist. National terrorists operate within the boundaries of a single nation in order to affect the issues related to that nation. Transnational terrorists operate in a specific region or worldwide to affect issues that impact numerous nations, regions, or globally.

Typical Profile of a Terrorist

While a terrorist can be anyone, there are some typical profiles that have emerged over the years. Generally, they have been male, between the ages of 22 and 28 years, unmarried, of urban origin and have a university level education. They have been upper middle class within their society and are often recruited from university, religious groups, and prison. For those taking part in terrorism and piracy in the waters between the Red Sea and the Indian Ocean, off the Somali coast, and into the

Strait of Malacca and Singapore the profile has been different. The difference is that these terrorists are mostly uneducated and are not considered middle class within their society.

Most foreign terrorists that are a threat to the United States and the maritime community are Marxist or Islamic Jihadist. Most domestic terrorists in the United States are antigovernment, Marxist, Islamic Jihadist, or racist groups and are also a threat to the maritime community.

Organizational Structure of Terrorist Groups

Each terrorist group can be organized differently; there are some common structures to these terrorist groups. Hard-core leadership is the management of the organization. These may include individuals or groups of individuals who control a particular terrorist organization.

The active cadre are the individuals in a terrorist organization who carry out the terrorist acts and collect intelligence for target selection. They are also involved in gathering logistic support in the field such as vehicles, weapons, and safe houses. The structure of the active cadre is that of small cells made up of four to six individuals. This is done for security reasons. The cells are organized by function, such as the intelligence cell that conducts intelligence missions for target selection. There are logistics cells that secure weapons, explosives, vehicles, and safe houses. The tactical cell carries out the terrorist activity.

Active supporters are individuals who provide support behind the scenes to the terrorist organization. These may include legal support, laundering of money, medical support, or political support.

Passive supporters are the useful idiots. They donate money, conduct fundraising, or take part in public demonstrations in support of their cause.

Operational Tactics

The operational tactics is how the terrorist carries out a method of attack. The most common tactic used at a shore facility is explosives. This tactic has also been used against vessels such as the USS Cole (DDG-67) guided missile destroyer on October 12, 2000 at the Yemeni port of Aden in which a suicide attack was carried out while it was harbored and being refueled. The attack killed 17 American sailors and injured 39. This allows the group to make a simple or complex explosive based on the funds and capabilities of the group members. There are numerous methods of activating an explosive device such as a timer, altimeter, light sensor, radio frequencies, pressure or trip wire, and suicide bombing. This allows the terrorist to escape capture or to die for their cause as a suicide bomber.

Assassinations are used to take out a specific target. This may be a political leader, law enforcement member, or any selected target. This was the case when the Irish Republic Army (IRA) targeted Lord Mountbatten while on holiday on his 30-foot vessel *Shadow V.* When the vessel was moored in the harbor at Mullaghmore, Ireland, a radio-controlled 50-pound explosive device was attached to it. On August 27, 1979 when the vessel was a few hundred yards from shore the bomb was detonated and assassinated Lord Mountbatten.

The hijacking of a vessel or taking individuals hostage or kidnapping, and armed assault are also tactics of terrorist groups. A recent case study was the 2009 hijacking of the first American cargo ship to be hijacked in 200 years since the formation of the U.S. Navy. The *MV Maersk Alabama* whose captain was Richard Phillips was hijacked by Somali pirates/terrorists ended when U.S. Navy Seals terminated the situation with no loss of innocent life.

Pirates and terrorists continue to use current technology. This includes the use of high-speed boats, automatic weapons, navigations, and communications systems to track and target ships. The new technology also allows the terrorist communicate with each other and the command or "mother ship" in a more effective manner.

Target Selection

The terrorist arena also improves their tactics and takes advantage of the vulnerable targets that include low-speed ships that are easy to approach. Ships that have a visible slow response to the perpetrators approach are targeted. Additional target attributes include ships with low freeboard for easy access. When targeting a ship, the terrorist will also look for a visible low state of alertness and a lack of any precautionary shipboard security measures. These are signs of inadequate security planning and procedures of the targeted vessels.

For shore-based operations, target selection involves choosing and identifying an individual, group of individuals, a port facility, or a ship at a port to strike. The terrorist groups seek a target that is soft, visible, and has high impact value.

A soft target is one that does not have a high level of security with easy access. An example would be the National Aquarium or business establishments located at the Baltimore Inner Harbor in Maryland (see Figures 2.3 and 2.4).

Unprotected ports and ships at port and lack of physical security and security force protection are considered a soft target; a visible target

FIGURE 2.3 National Aquarium at the Baltimore Inner Harbor, Maryland. (Photograph by Daniel J. Benny.)

FIGURE 2.4 Business establishments on the waterfront at the Baltimore Inner Harbor, Maryland. (Photograph by Daniel J. Benny.)

FIGURE 2.5   Three Mile Island Nuclear Plant on the Susquehanna River near Middletown, Pennsylvania. (Photograph by Daniel J. Benny.)

is one that is well known, such as a significant seaport, vacation cruise ship, or military vessel. Such a shore-based target could include the Three Mile Island Nuclear Plant located on the Susquehanna River near Middletown, Pennsylvania. It is famous for being the location of the most serious nuclear accident in the United States (see Figure 2.5).

A high impact target is one that will cause much damage or loss of life and will gain the media's attention. The destruction of a dam would cause enormous flooding and loss of life (see Figures 2.6 and 2.7).

Maritime terrorist attacks have the potential to inflict massive casualties and wreak economic havoc. All types of vessels such as passenger vessels, cruise ships, small commercial vessels, and private yachts that are susceptible to attack from terrorist organizations provide an opportunities for high death tolls, a key objective for Al-Qaeda and its Islamism terrorist affiliates. Attacks on large vessels such as container ships, oil tankers, and other oceangoing cargo ships would cause substantial damage to the global economy. Almost 90% of global trade travel is by sea. Attacks on oceangoing ships would raise risk levels, which would affect a number of trade factors that could result in higher prices for many commodities.

The threat of terrorism at sea raises new security concerns compared to traditional piracy. Pirates attack maritime targets for economic gain. As discussed previously, while terrorism attacks can be for an economic

FIGURE 2.6   A dam on the Susquehanna River in Pennsylvania—if breached by an act of terrorism would cause flooding and loss of life. (Photograph by Daniel J. Benny.)

FIGURE 2.7   Taking detailed photographs of the structure of Tower Bridge on the Thames River in London, England, could be a sign of terrorist surveillance. (Photograph by Daniel J. Benny.)

opportunity, most often the goal is to make a statement. The emerging threat is the use of weapons of mass destruction by terrorists in the maritime environment.

MARITIME TERRORISM AND WEAPONS OF MASS DESTRUCTION

Weapons of mass destruction (WMD) are weapons that have the capacity to inflict death and indiscriminate destruction on a massive scale. In the hands of a hostile power or terrorist organization such weapons are deadly. WMD can be nuclear/radioactive, biological, or chemical weapons.

Nuclear/Radioactive Weapons

Nuclear/radioactive weapons used by terrorist organizations may take on a variety of forms. If obtained by a terrorist group, a nuclear bomb or missile would be devastating. The weapon could be detonated at the surface level for maximum physical destruction or as an airburst creating an electromagnetic pulse that could destroy most of the communications and infrastructure in the area of its reach.

The nuclear threat may also be in the form of a dirty bomb. This is a traditional explosive device with radioactive material blended in with the explosive. When activated radiation spreads to the immediate area. This could be used against watercraft or a shore facility.

Radioactive material can be left in a public area at a shore facility or onboard a ship. This would contaminate individuals as well as the shore facility or ship that it was left on.

A nuclear attack may also be perpetrated by attacking a nuclear facility causing a meltdown of the radioactive core of the plant and the release of radiation to the public. There are many nuclear facilities located along coastal or navigable waterways that could be accessed from the water by terrorists using watercraft.

Biological Weapons

Biological weapons deliver toxins and microorganisms, such as viruses and bacteria, so as to deliberately inflict disease among people, animals, and agriculture. Biological attacks by a terrorist organization can result in the destruction of crops, disrupting communities and killing large numbers of people. Biological toxins can be absorbed through the skin and eyes, inhaled into the lungs, or ingested if food or water is contaminated. Attacks by terrorist organizations could be by transferring an agent, such as an aerosol that an unknowing target might inhale, or placing toxins in food or water supplies for ingestion onboard a cruise liner or any watercraft or shore facility.

What makes biological weapons so dangerous in most cases is that the target does not know they have been infected until symptoms begin to show. Symptoms may not appear for hours or days. Based on the type of agent used and the time it takes to appear during this period, other individuals can become infected resulting in mass casualties.

Chemical Weapons

Chemical weapons comprise a toxic chemical contained in a delivery system such as spray canister, explosive device, or artillery shell. This type of weapon based on the agent could cause death or injury to a large number of individuals. Unlike radioactive or biological attacks, if a chemical attack occurs, in most cases, it will be known immediately as the effect of the agent is felt once when they are inhaled, absorbed, or ingested into the body. Oftentimes, one can "see" or "smell" the agent, which gives people the opportunity to remove themselves from the danger by moving upwind from the attack. Chemical weapons could be used by a terrorist organization to attack a ship or shore facility.

THREAT RECOGNITION

The maritime community must be proactive to counter the threat of terrorism. As part of the maritime risk and threat analysis, the threat from terrorism must be calculated into that equation.

Intelligence is the key in assessing threats from terrorism and developing counterterrorism measures. Sources of intelligence for the maritime community would include the news and current events, liaison with local law enforcement agencies, the Transportation Security Administration, the U.S. Coast Guard, the International Association of Maritime Security Professionals, and security consultants.

Participation in the America's Waterway Watch program includes physical security measures, security awareness and training, and possible use of security forces based on the threat. The key is situational awareness. Establish a security-first conscious mind-set at all times. Develop 360° of protection starting from the perimeter of the shore-based property or hull of the ship working your way inward.

SIGNS OF TERRORISM

To counter terrorism, it is important to be alert to what is occurring at or around the marinas, port facilities, watercraft, and ships. There are some distinctive signs of possible terrorist activity against a general port or marina, which include the following:

- Surveillance
- Elicitation
- Test of security
- Acquiring supplies
- Suspicious people who do not belong
- Dry runs
- Deploying assets/getting into position

Surveillance

When terrorists have chosen a specific target, they will observe that area during the planning phase of the operation to gather intelligence. The goal is to determine the strengths, weaknesses, and number of personnel that may respond to an incident. Routes to and from the target are established during the surveillance phase. It is important to take note of activity where someone is recording or monitoring activities, drawing diagrams on or annotating maps, using vision-enhancing devices and/or having in one's possession floor plans or blueprints of port facilities and ships. Any of these surveillance-type acts are indicators that something is not right (see Figure 2.7).

Elicitation

The second sign is elicitation. This is when an individual attempts to gain information about the port or marina, a person, or tenant operations at the port or marina. An example is someone attempting to gain knowledge about the type of ship, fuel storage, or hours of staffing at the port facility. They may attempt to have individuals cleared to obtain Transportation Worker Identification Credentials so that they can place key people in sensitive work locations in part-time or full-time positions on the maritime property or as crew on yachts and ships.

Tests of Security

Tests of security are another area in which terrorists could attempt to gather information and intelligence about the port facility or watercraft.

This is conducted by driving by the target, moving into sensitive areas, and observing maritime security or law enforcement responses. Terrorists would be interested in the time in which it takes to respond to an incident and/or the routes taken to a specific location. They may also try to penetrate physical security barriers or procedures in order to assess strengths and weaknesses. They often gain legitimate employment at key locations in order to monitor day-to-day activities. In any event, they may try to gain this knowledge in order to make their mission or scheme more effective.

Acquiring Supplies

Another sign of terrorism to be cognizant of is anyone acquiring supplies. This may be a case where someone is purchasing or stealing explosives, weapons, or ammunition. It could also be someone storing harmful chemicals or chemical equipment. Terrorists could also find it useful to possess law enforcement equipment and identification, military uniforms, decals, and badges. If they cannot find the opportunity to steal these types of things, they may try to photocopy identification cards or attempt to make passports or other forms of identification by counterfeiting. Possessing any of these would make it easier for one to gain entrance into secured or usually prohibited areas.

Suspicious People Who Do Not Belong

A fifth pre-incident indicator is observing suspicious people who just do not belong. This does not mean we should profile individuals; rather, it means we should profile behaviors. It may mean someone at the maritime facility who does not fit in because of their demeanor, their language usage, or unusual questions they are asking.

Dry Runs

Another sign to watch for is dry runs. Before execution of the final operation or plan, a practice session may be conducted to work out the flaws and unanticipated problems. A dry run may very well be the heart of a planning stage of a terrorist act. If you find someone monitoring a marina on police radio frequency and recording emergency response times, you may very well be observing a dry run. Another element of this activity could include mapping out routes and determining the timing of vessel or vehicle traffic. This stage is the best chance to intercept and stop an attack. Multiple dry runs are normally conducted at or near the target area.

Deploying Assets/Getting into Position

The final sign to look for is someone deploying assets or getting into position. This is the last opportunity to alert authorities before the terrorist act occurs. It is also important to remember that pre-incident indicators may come months or even years apart. It is extremely important to document all information received no matter how insignificant it may appear and forward this information to the America's Waterway Watch program, Coast Guard, local law enforcement, the port facility management, and ship captains.

USE OF CRIMINAL PROFILING FOR COUNTER MARITIME TERRORISM

Criminal profiling is not new to law enforcement, intelligence, and security agencies and is a part of the investigative and intelligence process. It has been utilized in efforts to identify and apprehend individuals involved in various types of criminal activity such as serial murders, organized crime, drug cartels, and crimes related to illegal drugs, espionage, hate groups, and terrorist organizations.

When utilizing criminal profiling as an investigative tool, it is vital that law enforcement, intelligence, and security agencies base it on the facts of the case and not on bias or stereotyping. It needs to be based on objective data with numerous descriptive variables so that the range of offenders can be narrowed down.

It is important that law enforcement, intelligence, and security agencies not be restricted in performing their duties in identifying a suspect in terrorism because of political correctness. Criminal profiling is an accepted tool and should never be disregarded because of political correctness or because someone is offended.

Racial profiling is often confused with criminal profiling and in the minds of some it is one in the same. Racial profiling can be defined as investigating an individual or taking a law enforcement or security action against that individual based on an individual's race, national origin, religion, ethnicity, or sexual orientation.

Oftentimes what some would say is racial profiling is nothing more than the perception that it is occurring when in fact it was a clear case of the proper use of criminal profiling. In any event, some might say perceptions are everything. In the matter of offended feelings and misguided perceptions, they are not a justifiable reason to prohibit the law enforcement, intelligence, and security communities from performing their duties effectively in providing protection from terrorism through criminal profiling. In order to counter terrorism in the maritime community, criminal profiling can be a viable tool when properly utilized.

BIBLIOGRAPHY

International Maritime Organization. (2012). *Guide to maritime security and the ISPS code.* London, UK International Maritime Organization.

Mid-Atlantic Maritime Academy. (2012). *Vessel security officer.* Virginia Beach, VA: Mid-Atlantic Maritime Academy.

United States Coast Guard. (2002). *Maritime strategy for homeland security.* Washington, DC: U.S. Government Printing Office.

United States Coast Guard. (2014). *United States counter piracy and maritime security action plan.* Washington, DC: U.S. Government Printing Office.

United States Department of Homeland Security. (2008). *Small vessel security strategy.* Washington, DC: U.S. Government Printing Office.

CHAPTER 3

Cybersecurity Threats to the Maritime Community

CYBERSECURITY DEFINED

With the global use of Internet, an entire new area for attacks on the maritime profession has been created. The attacks against marinas, port facilities, and ships could be for the purpose of theft of property, information, or to circumvent security systems. It may be used to facilitate identity theft as well as the means to gather intelligence for terror activity. There is a possibility that cyberattacks may be used to disrupt the activity of a port or a ship. In order to know how to protect such information, the maritime community must have an understanding as to what the Internet is and the threats that may occur.

The Internet is an open, global network supporting standard utilities such as e-mail, file transfer, news groups, and the World Wide Web. The World Wide Web is a set of graphical, hyperlinked applications accessible over an organization's Internet. The Internet has opened a global communications medium and is used for internal communications, customer service and support, sales and distribution, electronic banking, marketing and research, and the storage of company confidential information as well as classified government information (see Figure 3.1).

There are several types of websites. The interactive site can be customized for the user and is primarily utilized for one-to-one communications. The transaction site allows account inquiry and online transactions.

Protection of the Internet and port or ship information is the end-system user's responsibility. The threat to the system and information can come from hackers, competitors, governments, customers, clients, contractors, or employees. They can wreak havoc on the organization's computer network through the destruction or modification of data as will be discussed in this chapter.

FIGURE 3.1 Personal computers must be considered with regard to Internet security. (Photograph by Daniel J. Benny.)

While most states have laws relating to computer crime, it is also a federal offense and falls under Title 18, Section 1030 and Title 18, Section 2701. The Federal Bureau of Investigation (FBI) has primary jurisdiction over all traditional investigations related to national defense, foreign relations, or any restricted data that can be used to cause damage to the United States. The U.S. Secret Service has primary jurisdiction over criminal acts involving consumer reporting. The FBI and U.S. Secret Service have concurrent jurisdiction over financial institution fraud.

THE THREAT FROM CYBERSECURITY ATTACKS

Adware

This software displays an advertisement on the target computer by the use of pop-ups. Once clicked, it can install itself on the computer, slowing the computer down and can also hijack the browser. The adware may also retrieve information from the computer or computer network and can be used for theft of information and intelligence gathering.

Anonymizing Proxies

If an employee or asset wants to hide their web browsing on a company's computer anonymizing proxies can be utilized. It also allows the user to bypass security filters that have been put in place.

AutoRun Worm

These malicious programs are able to access the computer through the Window AutoRun feature on the target computer. They most often can invade the computer with the introduction of a USB device to spread the AutoRun worm.

Chain Letters or E-Mail Malware

This is an e-mail letter that attempts to encourage the user to open the e-mail and forward it to other individuals. By clicking on the link, it will allow a virus or Trojan into the computer. It may also be used to spread rumors and false information harmful to the organization or send out e-mail under the company's name.

Cookies

A cookie is a file that is inserted onto the computer to allow the website to remember information on the user. This in itself is not a security issue. The concern is that it can also be used to track the browsing history of the user for commercial marketing but it is more important to obtain information for possible criminal and terrorist activity affecting the maritime community.

Data Theft, Leaks, and Loss

The unauthorized transfer of data and information from an organization's computer is called data theft, leak, or loss. This is one of the most common methods used for the theft of protected information on an organization or ship's computer.

Denial of Service

This is an attack on an organization's computer network in order to prevent the authorized user from accessing websites and information on the company's computer. This can be used to sabotage and disrupt an organization or ship's computer system.

Domain Name System Hijacking

The attacker changes the domain name setting so that it is ignored or controlled by another domain name. This allows unauthorized access to the computer and information.

Fraudulent Antivirus Malware

This alerts the computer user of a nonexistent virus in the computer so the user then clicks on the link, which allows a real virus into the computer, which can then be used to obtain protected information.

Internet Worms

This is a virus that when opened will reproduce itself across the local computer network and even on the Internet. It can infect computers beyond those of the targeted company or ship.

Keyloggers

This is a device that is plugged into the computer or downloaded into the computer and will record all keystrokes. The keylogger gives the asset the ability to identify the passwords on the computer. If the device is plugged into the computer, the perpetrator will then be able to return at a later time and log into the computer undetected using the stolen password. Use of the password will then make it appear that any retrieved information was accessed by the person whose password was stolen.

Mobile Phone Malware

This malware is designed to run on a mobile phone or smartphone in order to retrieve all of the information stored in the phone. This includes outgoing calls, phone numbers, text messages, photographs, and apps that have been accessed.

Phishing

This is the process of sending out a fraudulent e-mail representing a legitimate organization such as a bank or credit card company in an attempt to induce the target to provide sensitive information. This will allow the perpetrator to access accounts, computers, and other sources of information.

Social Networking Threats

With the use of social networking, there is the threat of theft of information or for a perpetrator to obtain sensitive information about a port or ship's activity. It may be from providing too much open source information on sites such as Facebook. Information can also be obtained on social sites from the use of pretext attempts to illicit information. Marina and port employees as well as boat owners, ship captains, and crews need to understand that any information placed on social media can be observed and used to facilitate a crime or terrorism. A phrase from the Office of Naval Intelligence used during World War II is still relevant today, "Loose lips sink ships."

Spyware

Spyware once installed on the computer allows those taking part in criminal activity to retrieve information from the computer or computer network.

Trojans

Trojans can be a serious threat that can enter the computer by disguising itself as a known software. Once downloaded on the computer, it will add itself to the computer start-up process. It can monitor everything on the computer and even generate e-mails from the infected computer.

COUNTERING MARITIME CYBERSECURITY ATTACKS

While developing a traditional loss prevention program you must conduct a risk assessment based on the projected use of the Internet and company computers. Computer security procedures need to be based on the greatest risk. To prevent unauthorized access, the computer security program should have at least two levels of protection. In keeping with Astor's Fifth Law of Loss Prevention, "any loss prevention control fails only upon audit." Ensure that there are strict monitoring and reporting procedures to support your security policy. Issues to consider are what services are allowed, what services or sites will be blocked, what is considered acceptable usage, and how will the policy be enforced.

As part of the protection plan, minimize and control the number of connections to the Internet. Increase the security of each connected computer and strengthen the network perimeter. The goal is to keep outsiders out, but allow insiders access to perform their assigned duties.

The key factors in the protection of marina, port, or ship's assets through the Internet are the development of a sound security policy and the use of proxy firewalls when possible. Ensure that the firewall software is up to date and examine the security of modem connections to avoid end runs. Conduct inspections and penetration testing software against the system.

By following these guidelines, the maritime community can reduce the threat of loss through the Internet at your marina, port facility, or ship.

The following are specific steps that can be taken to prevent the loss of protected information from cyberattacks against an organization's computers and computer network.

AntiMalware

This software can protect information on an organization's computer from attacks such as viruses, malware, worms, and Trojans. It scans the computer to identify programs that are not authorized. Once the malware is identified, it can be destroyed, eliminating the threat.

Anti-Spam

Anti-spam software can identify and prevent unwanted e-mail from reaching the in-boxes of an organization's computers. Most important is that many of these types of e-mails can be used to introduce viruses and malware into the system, which when opened can also be used to obtain protected information. Not only are annoying e-mails stopped but the potential for criminal activity is reduced as well.

Application Control

This is the process of blocking the use of identified applications that could compromise the security of a company's Internet system and information by the use of firewalls. This will not only prevent the loss of information but can also be used to prevent staff from operating unauthorized applications in the marina, port facility, or a ship's Internet system.

Encryption

Encryption is the coding of information sent, received, and stored to prevent unauthorized access and theft of sensitive information. The only fact was that the encryption can be read by an individual who is authorized and capable of decoding the encrypted information.

Firewalls

A network security system, a firewall acts as a barrier between computer networks to prevent malicious traffic that could damage or retrieve information, from obtaining access. In addition to preventing access, it can identify the threat and provide a warning that an attempt was made and has been blocked.

Intrusion Prevention Systems

This is a system that monitors all activity on a company's computer and provides notifications of threats or problems that it may identify. It is not only a preventive tool but it is also an investigative tool that can aid in the identification of the origin of the attack.

Network Access Control

This includes the authorization of those employees who are authorized to enter the system. It also includes the assessment of those trying to enter the system and the enforcement of company security policies.

ULR Content Filtering

This is utilized to block categories or specific websites that an organization does not want staff accessing from their company computers.

This not only prevents staff from browsing nonwork-related websites but also prevents viruses that may be introduced into the system when unauthorized websites are opened.

BIBLIOGRAPHY

Association of Certified Fraud Examiners. (2000). *Corporate espionage.* Austin, TX: Association of Certified Fraud Examiners.

United States Coast Guard. (2002) *Maritime strategy for homeland security.* Washington, DC: U.S. Government Printing Office.

CHAPTER 4

Components of Maritime Physical Security

Physical security measures need to be utilized as part of a comprehensive marina, port, and port facility security program. Physical security is also vital in the protection of small watercraft, yachts, and ships. Physical security will aid in the protection of life, sensitive information, property, as well as marina, port, port facility structures, small watercraft, yachts, and ships.

Note: This chapter will provide a generic overview of the components of a physical security program. The physical measures described can be used in various areas of maritime security. As specific areas of security are addressed in other chapters dealing with small watercraft, yachts, ships, marinas, port, and port facilities any unique physical security measures for each of those areas will be addressed in the related chapters.

The physical security sensors described are both current and some older technology. Older security sensors and systems are discussed as they may still be found at some maritime locations and can still be utilized as part of a total security system. If there are upgrades in the system and there is new construction, the most current technology and security sensors and system should be utilized.

The goals of physical security are to:

Deter entry: The use of signs, intrusion detection systems, barriers, locks, access control, metal detectors, x-ray, and security cameras can deter an individual(s) from taking part in criminal and terror activity.

Delay entry: Utilizing various physical security measures, should an individual not be deterred and attempt to take part in criminal activity, the physical security measures put in place can delay the perpetrator. During this period of delay, the perpetrator may be observed by a security officer, staff, the Coast Guard, or local law enforcement and the crime can be averted.

Detect entry: With the use of physical security devices, should an individual attempt to take part in criminal activity their presence and actions will be detected. This could result in the perpetrator stopping the criminal activity. It could result in the detection by security officers, or staff and apprehension by law enforcement. If a crime or loss of property is detected, management knows that there has been a threat and they can evaluate the adequacy of the current physical security system to prevent future threats.

Physical security also controls the movement of people such as employees, visitors, researchers, and vendors. Physical security measures can control access from entering and leaving the property, access to secured areas. Physical security also controls the movement of vehicles entering the property. They may be vehicles owned or driven be employees, visitors, or vendors.

INTRUSION DETECTION SYSTEMS

An intrusion detection system is designed to alert the monitoring station that someone has entered a protected area. This is accomplished through by a system of sensors that sends a notification to the computer base's monitoring stations or to a local sound-producing device when the sensor is activated. The intrusion detection system can be a proprietary central station in which it is monitored by security. It can also be a contract central station. The contract central station is a contract security monitoring service not located or associated with the property being protected. The contact central station receives the alarm and then notifies the police, fire, emergency medical services, the Coast Guard, local law enforcement, and the marina, port, or ship security departments on the type of alarm that is received.

The most common sensors are discussed in the following sections.

Electromagnetic Contacts

Electromagnetic contacts are used to provide protection for doors and windows. Contacts are placed on doors and doorframes or windows and windowsills. When a door or window is closed the contacts match together. When the alarm system is engaged, a current passes through the matching contacts. When a door or window is opened while the alarm is engaged, it breaks the circuit and the alarm is activated (Figure 4.1).

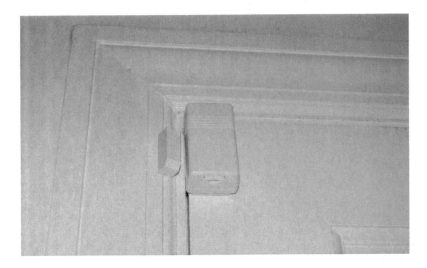

FIGURE 4.1   Electromagnetic sensor. (Photograph by Dr. Daniel J. Benny.)

Photoelectric Sensors

Photoelectric sensors are used to provide protection for doors and passageways or entrances to sensitive areas and are based on the principle of a light beam. When the light beam is broken by an individual, the alarm is activated. The photoelectric cell can also be used to automatically activate security lighting during periods of darkness.

Lasers

Lasers can provide protection for doors and passageways and is based on the principle a laser light beam. When the laser beam is broken, the alarm is activated. It can also be used to automatically activate security lighting during periods of darkness.

Glass Break Sensors

Glass break sensors are used on glass windows or glass-door areas to detect an attempted entry by breaking the glass. The sensor is mounted on the glass itself or near the glass window or door glass area and detects the vibration of the breaking glass.

Pressure Sensors

A pressure sensor is used to detect a person walking on a surface on the interior of a structure or the exterior grounds. The pressure-sensitive sensor is placed under the carpet inside of a property. If used outdoors it is buried under the surface of the ground. The alarm is activated when an individual walks over the surface where the sensor is concealed.

Vibration Sensors

Vibration sensors are used to provide protection in utility ports, which are large enough for an individual to access. When a perpetrator attempts to access an area that is protected by this sensor and touches the vibration sensor, it will activate the alarm.

Audio Sensors

An audio sensor is a microphone and in most cases a series of microphones that are placed inside the facility to be protected. Should there be an unauthorized access into the structure, the microphones are activated. The microphones can transmit all that is heard to a central station monitored by the property security department or at a contract central station. The security officer can then dispatch a response and notify the local police.

Ultrasonic Sensors

Ultrasonic sensors are used to protect the interior of a facility when it is not occupied. The sensor transceiver sends out sonar waves across the room that transverse back to the transceiver in a timed sequence. Should a perpetrator enter the protected area, the sonar waves are interrupted and the alarm is activated.

Microwave Sensors

A microwave sensor transceiver is used to protect the interior of a facility when it is un occupied. The sensor transceiver sends out microwaves across the room that transverse back to the transceiver in a timed sequence. Should a perpetrator enter the protected area, the microwaves

FIGURE 4.2 A microwave transceiver on the White House lawn, Washington, DC. (Photograph by Daniel J. Benny.)

are interrupted and the alarm is activated. This sensor should not be used in a room with large areas of glass as it will penetrate the glass and could result in false alarms. It may also be used to protect outdoor areas with restricted access (Figure 4.2).

Passive Infrared Sensors

The passive infrared sensor is the best monitoring transceiver to use for the interior protection of a facility when it is not occupied (Figure 4.3). The sensor transceiver sends out light energy that detects body heat. Should a perpetrator enter the protected area, the passive infrared detects the heat from the person, and the heat in the protected area, and the alarm is activated. This sensor is recommended.

Capacitance Proximity Sensors

Capacitance proximity sensors are used to protect metal safes and metal security containers. Once the sensor is attached to the safe or security container, a magnetic field around the protected item is established. The magnetic field will extend one foot around the protected safe or container. When a person walks into that space or touches the safe or container, their body will draw in the magnetism. This will cause a drop in the

FIGURE 4.3   Passive infrared sensor. (Photograph by Daniel J. Benny.)

magnetic field that is protecting the safe or security container and activate the alarm. This could also be used for a safe or steel key security container.

Sonar Sensors

These sensors can be deployed under the water to detect an unauthorized underwater approach to a marina, dock, and port facility. It can also be used to protect access to high-risk watercraft, yachts, and ships docked at port from underwater attacks.

FIRE DETECTION SYSTEMS

Almost all protection systems for marinas and port facilities will include intrusion detection and fire safety in one integrated system. The fire protection system can be activated manually with use of a "pull station" should one smell or see smoke and fire. The pull station will activate the audible and visual strobe fire protection annunciators in the building, and notify the central station and/or emergency dispatch to contact the fire department. In addition to the manual pull station, there is a fire protection sensor that can be placed in the facility that will send an automatic signal to the central station and/or emergency dispatch to contact the fire department and activate a set of the audible and visual strobe fire protection annunciators. The following fire protection sensors are available on the market.

Dual-Chamber Smoke Detectors

This sensor will provide early detection of smoke. It is used primarily for the protection of life, but early detection of a fire can also save property by providing early detection of a fire situation (Figure 4.4).

Rate of Rise Heat Detectors

This sensor is used in an area where a smoke detector cannot be used. This includes bathrooms and cooking areas and workshop-type areas where the normal activity would set off a smoke detector. The rate of rise heat detector will sense a rapid increase of heat in an area due to a fire and will then activate the alarm system.

FIGURE 4.4   Dual-chamber smoke detector. (Photograph by Daniel J. Benny.)

Natural Gas or Carbon Monoxide Detectors

These two types of sensors are used to detect deadly gases that may build up in a facility. These sensors provide an early warning for evacuation.

Waterflow Detectors

For facilities that have fire protection sprinkler systems, this sensor will detect a drop in water pressure when the sprinkler is activated during a fire. This will result in the activation of an alarm.

SECURITY CAMERAS

The use of security camera surveillance at ports and port facilities is very effective in the prevention of crime. It also allows for the documentation of events and provides evidence for an investigation should a crime occur. Security cameras can be utilized to provide protection from both external and internal theft (Figures 4.5 and 4.6).

Organizations may install security cameras at any location on the exterior of their property and in almost all interior areas. The areas where security cameras cannot be utilized are in restrooms and locker rooms.

FIGURE 4.5   Interior security camera. (Photograph by Daniel J. Benny.)

FIGURE 4.6   Exterior security camera. (Photograph by Daniel J. Benny.)

Other than those locations, there is no expectation of privacy in the work-place. Key areas for the placement of security cameras include entrances and exits to all property buildings, coverage of areas where valuable property, goods, and sensitive information is stored. There should be outdoor security camera coverage of parking areas and the grounds of port facilities by security cameras.

The components of a security camera system include the lens/camera, transmission of the signal, monitoring, and recording.

Lenses/Cameras

An effective security camera will require variable lens so that it is adaptable to low-light situations. This is critical for security coverage inside port facility structures and in low-light areas of docks. This allows for effective operations both during the day and night hours. It should be a color camera rather than a black-and-white camera in order to identify colors that are critical in security applications. It should be housed in a protective cover and have the ability to be operated remotely to allow for zoom, pan, and tilt.

Transmission of the Signal

The methods for transmitting a signal include the use of a coaxial cable, fiber optics, the Ethernet, microwave, RF radio, and laser. The best connection would be from a coaxial cable, fiber optics, or the Ethernet. In situations where a direct line cannot be used due to distance and other factors, microwave, RF radio, and laser can be used.

Monitoring

Observation of the camera image can be viewed on a traditional television screen that should have a resolution of no less than 512–491 pixels with 580 lines. It can also be viewed on a desktop or laptop computer screen.

Digital Recording and Monitoring

This can be accomplished with the use of a digital recording system. Digital recording provides the ability to store more information for a longer period of time depending on the server capacity. It also allows obtaining stills from the video and the ability to enhance and enlarge the stills for identification and to share with the U.S. Coast Guard and other law enforcement agencies. Another important feature of digital recording is that a time frame in the video can be searched by typing in the date and time period.

This makes retrieving and reviewing an important time event fast and easy. It can also be monitored remotely from a laptop computer (Figure 4.7).

Motion Detection

Security cameras can be equipped to work in conjunction with motion detection sensors that activate the recording of the view of the camera only during the time of activation by the motion sensor. The advantage of this is to save on the amount of recorded time on a VHS tape when using an analog system or space on a server when using a digital system. It is most often used during the investigation of internal theft when the security department only needs to view an area when the sensor was activated rather than going through hours of recordings.

FIGURE 4.7 Laptop computer used remotely to monitor digital security cameras at Long Level Marina in Wrightsville, Pennsylvania. (Photograph by Daniel J. Benny.)

Sonar placed underwater at ports can be used to activate an underwater security camera, should it be approached.

DETERMINING TOTAL SYSTEM COSTS

When determining the total cost for a security system, there are several categories that must be explored. These include the following:

- System design costs
- System installation costs
- System operational costs
- Maintenance costs
- IT costs
- Replacement costs
- Return on investment (ROI)

It is important in the development of a security system that the total cost of the system be attained in order to develop a realistic budget that can be justified to top management and ensure that the system installed meets the security requirements of the organization based on the threat.

System Design Costs

Initially, there is the cost to develop the specifications for the project. During this phase, it may require the assistance of a security consultant or engineer depending on the complexity and sophistication of the total security system.

During this phase, the examination of the requirements include the type of security system that would be the most effective based on the threat and location being protected and the various components of the system. These system components include the intrusion detection system central station server. It also includes the computer that would be utilized to operate the security system. The monitors that will be required to work the system must also be included in the system design. Depending on the size and number of monitors, it may require the construction of a rack system to hold the monitors.

The various types, numbers, and placement of the security sensors will need to be determined and documented. As an example, it would include electronic door contacts or passive infrared sensors. The number and placement of fire sensors including smoke detectors, heat detectors, and waterflow sensors also need to be determined.

Access controls such as card readers, cyberlocks and traditional locks and their placement in the facility must be identified. If electronic access control devices are utilized, conduit and wiring that are utilized to power the units will need to be calculated into the cost of the project.

The number and operating requirements of the security cameras will need to be identified. This will include the type of lenses, camera body, and operating aspects such as zoom capabilities and transmission methods. Conduit and wiring that are utilized to power the units will need to be calculated into the cost of the project and that will be integrated into the total security system that is being planned.

The design cost also includes the development of the drawings and blueprints of the total system to be constructed and installed. There are, of course, the consultant fees for the individual or firm that is hired to design the security system. Costs for the engineer or engineering firm who will create the drawings and blueprints of the project must also be considered in the design process.

There are many aspects of the system design cost that must be taken into account. This will be important when submitting a budget for such a project. The life cycle of the security system should also be a consideration for long-term budget projection.

System Installation Costs

One of the most expensive aspects of an entire security system project is the system installation cost. This includes the cost of the products or components of the security system such as the following:

- Server
- Computers
- Monitors
- Control panels
- Wiring
- Metal conduits
- Security cameras
- Camera brackets and housing

There is also the expense of the various sensors such as door and window contacts, motion sensors, and fire protection sensors integrated into the system. If access control is part of the system, then there is the cost of the readers and cards to be used with the product.

Once the products have been identified and purchased, there will be shipping costs to transport the system components to the installation site. This could include fees for rail and truck transport of large parts and the cost of local carriers for smaller products associated with the security system.

Labor costs for the individuals installing the system can be sizeable based on the union or nonunion wages in the local area. This could include electricians and any construction that may be required to support the security system. It may also include masons, carpenters, and painters.

Permits are required in most cases for new construction and electrical installations from the local government or municipality. The cost of permits will vary based on these local governments and their specific requirement in which the facility and the security system project is located. Based on the nature of the product, there may also be state or Environmental Protection Agency permit fees.

System Operational Costs

Once the system is installed, there will be initial and ongoing system operation costs.

In order to ensure the proper function of the system, current policies will need to be rewritten as well as the writing of new policies with regard to the operation of the security system. These operational changes may impact how other departments in an organization operate, causing additional costs to make such changes to the company's operating policy and infrastructure.

Since all new security systems are computer based, there will be significant initial and ongoing support from an organization's IT department. This includes integrating the security system into the company IT system, the development of IT security procedures, and software to protect the system.

The increase in cost for electrical power is also part of the system operating cost.

In the event of a power loss, the security system must function so an emergency backup generator must be included in the ongoing cost.

The most expensive ongoing cost will include initial and continued training of the security staff and the wages for additional security staff that will monitor the security system. In some cases, the addition of a comprehensive security system may free some security officers on patrol to monitor the system, but this is not the norm. In most situations, additional security will need to be hired.

IT-Related Costs

When developing a new security system that is computer based, there will be IT-related costs. It is vital to know what IT systems are available on the corporate IP network. In the total cost of the security system, you will need to account for these cost factors associated with industry's best practices for the management of IP-based technologies such as

- Antivirus technology
- System patches
- Database management
- Backup and archiving
- Network bandwidth and quality of service

Each of these costs will have an associated cost for labor and IT personnel who may be dedicated partly or fully to monitoring and maintaining the new systems.

Maintenance Costs

Keeping the system operating will require an investment in ongoing maintenance. This includes routine costs to keep the system's hardware running and upgrades to the software. It will also require updates to the physical components of the system such as wiring and mechanical functions.

If the system goes down in an emergency situation, there will be emergency repair and labor costs, especially if it were to be during the evening, weekends, or on a holiday when labor rates are higher. There will also be the labor cost for additional security and management staff to provide security coverage if the security system is not operating.

One method of reducing the cost to routine and emergency labor is to enter into an annual maintenance contract. It will often allow for a reduced rate for monthly or quarterly work on the security system, as well as emergency maintenance situations during the day, evenings, weekends, or holidays.

Replacement Costs

All things must pass and that is true of security systems that become inoperable or antiquated. When designing and installing a new system, it is important to determine the life of the system. How long it will last before it needs to be replaced or becomes obsolete based on new hardware or software.

The manufacturer can most often advise on the life cycle of the system and potential future changes that may occur along with a time frame for such changes. Based on the life expectancy projection, a long-term budget should be established so that there are funds for the replacement of the security system at the anticipated replacement time.

The life cycle of the security system should also be a consideration when a system is first selected.

Cost–Benefit Analysis

When developing a security system, stakeholders must often prioritize requirements as part of the engineering process. Not all aspects may be implemented due to lack of time, lack of resources, or changing or unclear project goals. It is important to define which requirements should be given priority over others.

Cost of Loss

Computing the cost of a security system can be very difficult. A simple cost calculation can take into account the cost of repairing or replacing the security system. A more sophisticated cost calculation can consider the cost of having the security system out of service, added training, additional procedures resulting from a loss, the cost to a company's reputation, and clients. For most purposes, you do not need to assign an exact value to each possible risk. Normally, assigning a cost range to each item is sufficient. One method for analyzing the cost is to assign these costs based on a scale of loss as follows:

- Nonavailability of security system over a short term (7–10 days)
- Nonavailability of security system over a medium term (1–2 weeks)
- Nonavailability of security system over a long term (more than 2 weeks)
- Permanent loss or destruction of the security system
- Accidental partial loss or damage of the security system
- Deliberate partial loss or damage of the security system
- Unauthorized disclosure within the organization
- Replacement or recovery cost of the security system

Cost of Prevention

This includes calculating the cost of preventing each type of loss. This could include the cost to recover from

- Fire
- Power failure
- Terrorist incident

Costs need to be amortized over the expected lifetime of the security system.

Return on Investment

In all areas of management it is important to include the development of a total security system. Return on investment (ROI) is a critical step in selling the system to top management and obtaining funds for the project.

A security investment such as a physical security system can enhance the security picture and improve the financial picture of an organization. Many security professionals have the technical security knowledge to sell a security system to top management but lack the ability to show how security improvements can contribute to a company's profitability.

When making a business case for a total security system investment that will include software or hardware, it is imperative to accurately capture the costs and benefits, and present the results in compelling financial terms. Knowledge on how to quantify the security investment and the projected return in ways that top management and other financial stakeholders are used to seeing can be critical to obtaining endorsement of the security system.

ROI is a concept used to maximize profit to an organization for money spent. It is used to determine the security system's financial worth. ROI is the annual rate of return on an investment.

Developing a security system can be complex. ROI can be measured using two basic criteria: costs and benefits. The object is to establish a credible ROI and also to define a high-value security system project by the benefits that it provides.

It is important to identify the purpose of the security system project. Is the project worth it? Will it improve security? If you can answer yes the next decision is the priority of the security system project in the scheme of the total organizational goals. While security risk needs to be a priority, financial factors are a reality. Fiscally responsible planning and prioritizing will weigh in the project's favor in the decision-making process. The description of the project's purpose should include a clear statement for the need of the security system. It is important to capture all the relevant costs of a project as it relates to ROI.

Total cost of ownership (TCO) is the cost to an organization to acquire, support, and maintain the security system. TCO can be articulated this way:

$$TCO = \text{cost to buy} + \text{cost to install} + \text{cost to operate} + \text{cost to maintain}$$

Cost Factors

Three are common cost factors associated with the development of a security system. It is vital to estimate both the extent and timing of costs to be incurred during the security systems project.

Typical cost factors for security systems may include the following:

Security Cameras/Video

- Cameras
- Encoders
- Fiber transceivers
- Monitors
- VCR-DVR-NVR
- Mass storage

Access Control

- Panels
- Doors and locks
- Readers
- Gates
- Other security sensors

Communications

- Leased line costs
- Costs associated with interoperability of systems

Cabling and Power Supplies

Personnel associated with the security system

- Receptionist
- Credentialing
- Contractor administration
- Lock and key management

Monitoring and Control Rooms

- Alarm and video monitoring personnel
- Operations support personnel
- Physical security information management systems
- Awareness and response systems

General System-Related Costs

- Engineering and design
- Infrastructure and maintenance
- Software and licensing
- System deployment
- Application integration
- Administration and troubleshooting
- User training

To be successful in selling the project you must identify the benefits as they relate to ROI. Start with the direct benefits, which are verifiable and easy to understand. Indirect benefits can be selectively included later if they contribute to the ROI.

The ROI can be justified based on the *direct benefits* attributable to the security system project. Direct benefits may include the following:

- Space improvements
- Wiring and communications infrastructure improvements
- Servers, applications, or system improvements
- Storage increase
- Integration of systems such as security, fire protection, access control
- System maintenance and upgrades
- Training improvements

Indirect benefits are not easily measured. Productivity improvement is an example of an indirect benefit. Since indirect benefits may involve some subjectivity, separating indirect and direct benefits makes a proposal evaluation easier, increasing the chances of receiving thorough consideration. IP-based physical security can be used to increase efficiency and provide labor reduction. The following list is an example of *indirect benefits* or solutions.

- Visitor management administration and control
- Segregation of duties
- Parking permit administration
- Property pass administration
- Employee timekeeping
- System troubleshooting and maintenance
- Alarm correlation and response
- Emergency communication and notification

Once the cost and benefit data are collected, they must be analyzed to determine the ROI. This can be accomplished by using the TCO comparisons as shown earlier.

The ROI should be presented in a clear and concise executive summary. Presenting the ROI of the proposal in this manner can lead to the approval of the security system.

Capturing this advantage in quantifiable and credible terms will permit the calculation of ROI. In the current business climate, it is crucial to justify the expenditure for a security system even if the risk shows that it is vital to the security of the organization. By using the ROI model demonstrates the security director's business acumen and sensitivity to resource limitations. This will build the security manager's credibility with top management.

Determining the total security system cost is an important aspect for the development of the proposed security system. It aids in the approval and funding for the security system project by top management.

LOCKS, KEY CONTROLS, AND ACCESS CONTROLS

The use of locks is one of the oldest forms of security. There are two general categories of locks: those that operate on mechanical concepts and those that use electricity to operate mechanical components of the locking system. Locks are used to secure personnel doors, ships hatches, windows, utility ports, gates, file cabinets, and security containers in the protection of people, artifacts, books, and collections.

In addition to preventing access based on security concerns, locks can also prevent access to areas for safety-related issues. This might include securing hazardous materials storage areas, electrical rooms, engine rooms, and to lock equipment on/off switches.

Mechanical Locks

A mechanical lock utilizes physical moving parts and barriers to prevent the opening of the latch and includes the following: the latch or bolt that holds the door or window to the frame. The strike is the part into which the latch is inserted. The barrier is a tumbler array that must be passed by use of a key to operate the latch. The key is used to pass through the tumbler array and operated the latch or bolt.

Wafer Tumbler Locks

This lock utilizes flat metal tumblers that function inside the shell of the lock housing that creates a shear line. A spring tension keeps each wafer locked into the shell until lifted out by the key. The shell is matched by varying bit depths on the key (see Figure 4.8).

FIGURE 4.8   Low security wafer tumbler padlock. (Photograph by Daniel J. Benny.)

Dial Combination Locks

The dial combination lock is used on security containers, safes, and vaults and is opened by dialing in a set combination. By eliminating a keyway, it provides a higher level of security. While these locks do not utilize a key, they work on the same principle as the lever lock. By aligning gates on tumblers to allow insertion of the fence in the bolt, the lock can be opened by dialing in the assigned combination. The number of tumblers in the lock will determine the numbers to be used to open the combination lock.

High-Security Deadbolt Locks

A deadbolt lock is utilized for securing exterior and interior doors (Figures 4.9 through 4.12).

The elements of high-security deadbolt locks are the use of a restricted keyway so that the key cannot be easily duplicated, a 1-inch latch with

FIGURE 4.9   Electronic keypad lock. (Photograph by Daniel J. Benny.)

FIGURE 4.10   Security lock. (Photograph by Daniel J. Benny.)

FIGURE 4.11   Deadbolt lock. (Photograph by Daniel J. Benny.)

FIGURE 4.12   Deadbolt lock with a safety chain. (Photograph by Daniel J. Benny.)

ceramic inserts so that the latch cannot be forced open or cut; tapered and rotating cylinder guards should be used so that a wrench cannot be used to remove the lock.

Card Access Electrified Locks

Electrified locks permit doors to be locked and unlocked in a remote manner (Figures 4.13 and 4.14). It can be a simple push button near the lock or at a security central station or as part of a card proximity reader system or digital keypad. This system allows for the use of traditional electric latches or can be used with an electric high-security deadbolt system.

Exit Locks

Exit locks or panic bars are used on doors designed as emergency exits from a building (Figure 4.15). They are locked from the outside but can be opened to exit the building by pushing on a bar that disengages the lock. Emergency doors should never be locked from the inside in any manner, which would not allow for immediate exit from the building.

FIGURE 4.13   Proximity card reader. (Photograph by Daniel J. Benny.)

FIGURE 4.14   Proximity card reader on a turnstile to control personnel access to a maritime facility. (Photograph by Daniel J. Benny.)

FIGURE 4.15   Emergency door locking system. (Photograph by Daniel J. Benny.)

Master Locking Systems

When establishing a master locking system, it must be designed to meet the security needs of the marina or vessel. Without planning, the locking system will usually degrade to a system that is only providing privacy but not effective security. The goal is to make the locking system effective and user friendly so that the functions of the marina, port, and ship can continue unimpeded.

The number of locks needs to be considered in the development of a master locking system. This includes the total number of locks that will be installed on a marina facility's exterior and interior doors. The categories of a locking system include exterior doors entering a building on a property, interior doors, and high-security areas; combination locks for security containers and safes; and cabinet locks for desks, computers, and file cabinets.

Control of Keys and Locking Devices

The security department, if there is one, or the port or marina manager should control all keys and locking devices. This includes the responsibility for the installation and repair of all locks, as well as maintaining the records of all keys made, issued, and collected.

Master Keys

The master key is a single key that fits all locks and must be controlled and secured by the security department or manager and should not be removed from the property. This key may be *signed out* to members of the staff. It should only be issued each day and needs to be signed for and returned at the end of the shift when the security staff or top management leaves for the day. Submaster keys that allow access to specific areas of the port or marina may be issued for the term of employment to top management or security staff. The security department should also keep a duplicate of all keys to the facility, desks, file cabinets, and access numbers to combination locks on security containers.

Duplication of Keys

The duplication of company keys must be controlled. No key should be duplicated by the authorized locksmith without the authorization by the management or the security department.

Lost Keys

Lost or misplaced keys should be reported at once. An investigation in the circumstances related to the loss or misplacement of keys must be conducted.

Disposition of Employee Keys upon Transfer or Termination

Upon the transfer of an employee or the termination of an employee, all keys that were issued must be returned and accounted for. This would include door, desk, and file cabinet keys issued to the employee.

SECURITY CONTAINERS

When protecting sensitive information, it is vital to have the documents or media stored in security containers or safes. These security containers should be of high-quality commercial products (see Figure 4.16).

When protecting U.S. government classified information, the security containers and safes must meet U.S. General Services Administration

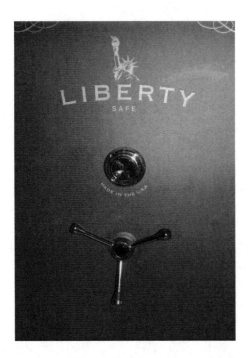

FIGURE 4.16   Commercial liberty safe. (Photograph by Daniel J. Benny.)

(GSA) standards and approval. All security containers that are approved by the GSA will bear a General Services Administration Approved Security Container label affixed to the front of the security container and are classified as follows:

Class 1

The security container is insulated for fire protection. And the protection provided is

- 30 man-minutes against surreptitious entry
- 10 man-minutes against forced entry
- 1-hour protection against fire damage to content
- 20 man-hours against manipulation of the lock
- 20 man-hours against radiological attack

Class 2

The security container is insulated for fire protection and the protection provided is

- 20 man-minutes against surreptitious entry
- 1-hour protection against fire damage to contents

- 5 man-minutes against forced entry
- 20 man-hours against manipulation of the lock
- 20 man-hours against radiological attack

Class 3

The security container is uninsulated and the protection provided is

- 20 man-minutes against surreptitious entry
- 20 man-hours against manipulation of the lock
- 20 man-hours against radiological attack
- No forced entry requirement

Class 4

The security container is uninsulated and the protection provided is

- 20 man-minutes against surreptitious entry
- 5 man-minutes against forced entry
- 20 man-hours against manipulation of the lock
- 20 man-hours against radiological attack

Class 5

The security container is uninsulated and the protection provided is

- 20 man-hours against surreptitious entry (increased from 30 man-minutes on containers produced after March 1991)
- 10 man-minutes against forced entry
- 20 man-hours against manipulation of the lock
- 20 man-hours against radiological attack
- 30 man-minutes against covert entry

Class 6

The security container is uninsulated and the protection provided is

- 20 man-hours against surreptitious entry
- No forced entry test requirement
- 20 man-hours against manipulation of the lock
- 20 man-hours against radiological attack
- 30 man-minutes against covert entry

Security Filing Cabinets

A variety of security filing cabinets are manufactured to meet the standards of the Class 5 and Class 6 security containers. Security filing cabinets are available in a variety of styles to include single, two, four, and five drawers and in both letter size and legal size models.

SECURITY BARRIERS AND FENCING

A security barrier can be anything that prevents vehicle or pedestrian access to the property or the facility and protected information. It may be natural barriers such as water, trees, or rock formations. One of the natural barriers that ports have from at least one access point is the water. These natural barriers may already be in place or can be placed on the property to provide a natural barrier (Figures 4.17 and 4.18). This is one of the aspects of what is known as Crime Prevention Through Environmental Design (CPTED).

One of the most cost-effective security barriers used to secure the perimeter of a property is chain link fencing (Figure 4.19). Chain link fencing is relatively low in cost and provides the flexibility to move it as needed. It also allows visibility beyond the property line by security, staff, and security cameras.

Chain link fencing cannot be used at some facilities because they are not aesthetically pleasing to look at. They may also be used for some outdoor storage areas. Decorative fencing is often more aesthetically appealing and can provide adequate perimeter security (Figure 4.20).

FIGURE 4.17   Alcatraz Island, San Francisco, California, has water as a natural barrier. (Photograph by Daniel J. Benny.)

FIGURE 4.18 Three Mile Island Nuclear Power Plant, Middletown, Pennsylvania, has water as a natural barrier. (Photograph by Daniel J. Benny.)

FIGURE 4.19 Chain link fencing at Lakeside Marine, Harrisburg, Pennsylvania. (Photograph by Daniel J. Benny.)

FIGURE 4.20 Decorative fencing at one of the White House gates, Washington, DC. (Photograph by Daniel J. Benny.)

The security industry height for the fence is 6 feet with a 1-foot top guard mounted at a 45° angle facing away from the property constructed of barbed wire or razor ribbon. The fence must be secured in the ground by metal posts with bracing across the top and bottom of the fence. The opening in the fence should be no more than 2 inches.

With any fencing that is utilized for areas with vehicle access, there should be at least two points of access in the event that one access is closed due to an emergency. All gates that are not used on a regular basis need to be secured with a high-security padlock. The locked gate should also be equipped with a numbered security seal. This seal needs to be checked each day by security or port/marina staff to ensure that the numbered seal is intact and matches the numbered seal placed on the gate. This is to ensure that an unauthorized key is not being used. It is also used to ensure that the original padlock on the gate was not cut off and replaced with a different lock and then used by a perpetrator for continued unauthorized access into the secure area.

Access onto the property through the gate can be controlled by the use of a proximity access card and electric locking system on the gate. This can be used for vehicles or individuals.

Security fencing or netting can also be utilized underwater near docks and ships to prevent underwater access to facilities and watercraft. The underwater netting may be used for long-term or only during short-term high-risk situations or threat levels.

FIGURE 4.21 Hydraulic vehicle barrier used at 10 Downing Street, London, England, to prevent unauthorized vehicle access to the residence of the British Prime Minister. (Photograph by Daniel J. Benny.)

Vehicle barriers can be used in conjunction with fencing and access control to prevent a vehicle from ramming through an access point (see Figure 4.21).

SECURITY LIGHTING

Security lighting is used to illuminate the perimeter of the property, gate access area, walkway, and the vehicle parking area of a facility. The most effective security lighting is sodium vapor lights (Figure 4.22).

Lighting fixtures need to be placed in a security housing to prevent damage. The light can be mounted on posts and buildings. Lights can be activated by the use of a photoelectric cell that will automatically turn the light on at dusk and turn it off at dawn. This is more efficient than manually turning lights on and off each day. At ports, the security lighting must not be placed in a manner that would be confusing to or interfere with U.S. Coast Guard aids to navigation.

All light fixtures should be numbered and identified for easy identification. This will be of value when reporting lights that are not working to ensure that they are repaired as quickly as possible.

FIGURE 4.22   Exterior security and emergency lighting at a port facility. (Photograph by Daniel J. Benny.)

These types of lighting devices include the following:

- Incandescents
- New fluorescents (to replace the incandescent)
- Quartz lighting
- Mercury vapor lights
- Sodium vapor lights

Incandescents

This is what is known as the common light bulb or floodlight that is being phased out. It has been used to provide illumination at doorways and to direct light toward a building at night. It is suitable for security for a single building, but is not considered for security lighting of large facilities. This is due to the high-energy cost and low illumination that it provides.

Quartz Lighting

Quartz lighting provides better illumination and emits a white light. It is activated instantaneously when turned on and has been used to light parking areas. It does have a high energy cost.

Mercury Vapor Lights

The mercury vapor light provides good illumination and emits a white light. It does require a warm-up time and cannot be activated instantaneously when turned on. It is used to light parking areas and roadways. It has a lower energy cost than the previously mentioned lights.

Sodium Vapor Lights

The sodium vapor light is considered the best for security. It will light instantaneously and has a lower energy cost than all other security lighting. It has excellent penetration at night and in fog due to the amber light. The amber light can distort color on security cameras and upon viewing objects by security officer.

PROTECTION OF WINDOWS AND UTILITY PORTS

All port facilities have windows that will require protection. The first security consideration for window protection is the window itself or what is called glazing. That is the type of glass or plastic that is used as a window. The more security that is required, the stronger the glazing should be. The stronger the glazing, the more expensive it will be. What is used will be based on the threat assessment and if there are any interior intrusion detection systems being used in the structure.

Window areas can be made of glass, acrylic, or what is known as Lexan. The following is a list of the glass, acrylic, and Lexan products that can be used for nonbullet-resistant protection:

- Annealed glass
- Wire-reinforced glass
- Tempered glass
- Laminated glass
- Annealed glass—with a security film
- Acrylic
- Lexan

Annealed Glass

Of all the glazing materials, annealed glass, also known as windowpane glass, breaks very easily and provides the least amount of protection. It breaks into shards of glass that are very sharp and can be used as a weapon. These shards can cause injury to individuals in the area if the glazing material is broken by a perpetrator or explosive blast.

Wire-Reinforced Glass

Wire-reinforced glass is an annealed glass with wire imbedded into the glazing. While it looks as if it adds security, it does not and can be easily broken. The one advantage is that the glass does not break in large shards as the wire holds the broken glass together.

Tempered Glass

Tempered glass is a stronger material, but can be defeated easily. When broken, it breaks into small pieces of glass that are relatively harmless. This glass was used in older vehicle windshields.

Laminated Glass

Laminated glass is coated with a plastic. It can also be defeated easily. When broken, it holds the glass together in large harmless sheets. This is why it is used in vehicle windshields.

Annealed Glass with a Security Film

Annealed glass with a security film has a layer of acrylic between two layers of glass. It is difficult to break through this glazing and is the best of the glass products for security protection when bullet resistance is not a requirement.

Acrylic

Acrylic is a plastic and offers little protection. It also breaks into large shards if broken. It can also scratch easily and will discolor over time due to sunlight.

Lexan

Lexan is a trademark name of a glazing that is impregnable to breakage and is the best of all the security glazing when bullet resistance is not a requirement.

Where bullet resistance is required due to a high threat of robbery or terrorist attack by firearms or explosive devices, the following bullet-resistant material can be utilized:

- Bullet-resistant glass
- Bullet-resistant acrylic
- Lexgard

Bullet-Resistant Glass

Bullet-resistant glass is a glass glazing that can be from ¼ to 1 inches in thick. The thicker the glass, the more protection it provides from small-arms weapons. It will stop most bullets, but it does cause spalling. Spalling is when a bullet is trapped in the glass, and a small particle of glass breaks off and flies in the direction away from where the bullet was fired. This can cause injury to any one who is near the bullet-resistant glass.

Bullet-Resistant Acrylic

Bullet-resistant acrylic is an acrylic glazing that can be from ¼ to 1 inch thick. The thicker the glazing, the more protection it provides from small-arms weapons. It will stop most bullets but it can cause spalling.

Lexgard

Lexgard is the trademark name of an acrylic glazing (Figure 4.23). A 1-inch thick glazing is the best protection from firearms and explosive devices and will stop all small-arms weapons and most rifles. With Lexgard, there will be no spalling. This is a product that one would find on the presidential limousines used by the U.S. Secret Service.

Window protection can also be provided with the use of security bars or steel screening placed over the windows. The bars and screens should

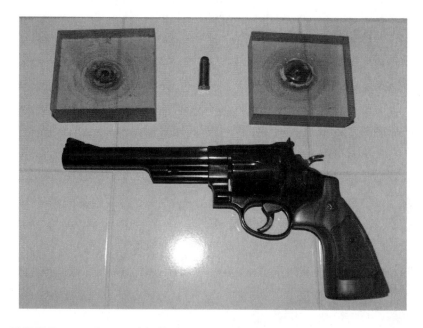

FIGURE 4.23 Lexgard bullet-resistant glazing shot with a .44 Magnum Smith & Wesson. (Photograph by Daniel J. Benny.)

be securely mounted into the window frame. It is important to ensure that the use of bars and steel screens on the windows do not impede emergency access out of the structure in the event of an emergency evacuation.

Utility ports are areas of access into port facilities such as water, air vents, and trash. These areas can be protected with bars, locks, and intrusion detection systems. The use of security cameras is also recommended for trash compactor areas.

RADIO FREQUENCY IDENTIFICATION, MAGNETOMETERS, AND X-RAYS

Physical security measures can be of value in the protection of property when used at the entrances and exits of property. The concept is to use a security device that is placed on the materials to be protected and to have security detection as well as a detection device that is typically located at all exits. The detection devices must be safe for magnetic media and usually have audible and/or visible alarms.

There are two primary methods currently used for detection: electromagnetic detection and radio frequency identifications (RFID) (Figure 4.24). These technological solutions can prevent, reduce, and detect the theft of property. Of the two methods, the most effective is the radio

FIGURE 4.24   Electromagnetic detection system. (Photograph by Daniel J. Benny.)

frequency identification. The advantage of this system is that it does not require line-of-sight to be read. The tags can be placed on any type of property or media, including CDs, DVDs, and videocassettes. A portion of the RFID memory can be allocated for theft protection so that no other tag is required. Since the antitheft device is located within the label, the security gates do not need to be attached to a central system or interface with the property central database.

Magnetometers

Used at entrances and exits of a property, a magnetometer, also known as a metal detector, is a physical security device that responds to metal that may not be readily apparent by direct observation. The simplest form of a metal detector consists of an oscillator producing an alternating current that passes through a coil producing an alternating magnetic field. If a piece of electrically conductive metal is close to the coil, eddy currents will be induced in the metal, and this produces an alternating magnetic field of its own. As part of the security system when another coil is used to measure the magnetic field, acting as a magnetometer, the change in the magnetic field due to the metallic object can be detected.

This can be used to detect the removal of metal objects from the property or from individuals bring items in side of the port facilities such as weapons or tools that could be used to defeat a physical security system once inside the port facility.

X-Rays

X-rays are is used at entrances and exits of a property to inspect cases, handbags, or packages entering or leaving the property. It is used to detect contraband, weapons, explosives entering the facility or items being removed. The use of x-rays in most cases will deter such activity and can of course detect such attempts.

BIBLIOGRAPHY

Baker, P., & Benny, D. J. (2012). *Complete guide to physical security.* Boca Raton, FL: CRC Press.

Fischer, R. J., & Green, G. (2012). *Introduction to security* (9th ed.). Burlington, MA: Elsevier.

International Maritime Organization. (2012). *Guide to maritime security and the ISPS code.* London, UK: International Maritime Organization.

United States Department of Homeland Security. (2008). *Small vessel security strategy.* Washington, DC: U.S. Government Printing Office.

United States Power Squadron/University of West Florida. (2012). *USPS University/ University of West Florida Seminar Small Boat Security.* Pensacola, FL: University of West.

CHAPTER 5

Security Departments

Note: As with a chapter on physical security, this coverage of security departments will be a generic overview. How such security forces are utilized at marinas, ports, port facilities, and on yachts and ships will be described in the chapters that address those specific areas of the maritime community.

CHIEF SECURITY OFFICER

When establishing a security department, the hiring of a security professional such as the Chief Security Officer (CSO) is the first priority. The selection of this individual is critical to the success of the operation of the security department. The CSO should report to the Chief Executive Officer or top management of the marina or port facility and is shipboard to the ship's captain. The individual selected should have at a minimum a bachelor's degree from an accredited university or college in Security Administration or Criminal Justice with a Master or Doctorate degree preferred.

A security professional with professional security certification should also be considered. There are several security-related certifications that would be of value to the CSO. The certification is offered by the American Society for Industrial Security International (ASIS International). ASIS International has developed a professional security certification known as the Certified Protection Professional (CPP). This designation is accepted nationally and internationally by the security profession as well as the U.S. Homeland Security, the U.S. Coast Guard, and the Transportation Security Administration.

The CPP has been established for individuals working in security supervision and management. Upon successful completion of the comprehensive exam, one must have a combination of years of security management experience or college degrees.

The International Association of Maritime Security Professionals established the Certified Maritime Security Professional (CMSP) designation for those working specifically in the maritime security profession. To earn the designation, the candidate must have positive references, 5 years of experience in maritime security, pass a certification exam, and agree to follow the code of values and ethics of the International Association of Maritime Security Professionals.

DETERMINING THE SIZE OF THE SECURITY DEPARTMENT

Once the CSO is hired, he or she must work with the Chief Executive Officer or ship's captain to make a determination with regard to the size of the security department that will be required. The need for a security department must be established and will be based on several factors.

These factors include a physical security survey of the maritime property or ship to be protected by the security department. The duties and functions of the security department at the maritime or ship property must be considered based on the security threat.

The physical security survey and the physical security measures to be utilized at the maritime property will have an impact on the number of security officers who will be required to provide adequate protection.

The use of intrusion detection systems, security cameras, security lights, fire protections systems, and access control such as proximity card readers may reduce the number of security officers required to patrol the maritime property or ship. If there are no or limited physical security measures, there will be a requirement to establish a larger security force in order to effectively secure the location to be protected. The use of more physical security measures may allow for the reduction of the size of the force. Regardless of the level of physical security protection, there will in most cases be a need for security officers to monitor the intrusion detection system, fire, access control, and camera systems. There is also the requirement for security officers to be able to respond to the various alarms or activity observed on security cameras.

For each security post to be covered 24 hours a day, the maritime organization would need to hire four security officers to account for days off, holidays, and vacations. So, if two security officers are required to be on duty 24 hours a day, there would be a requirement to hire eight security officers.

MISSION OF THE SECURITY DEPARTMENT

When making a decision on the size of a security force, the mission and duties of the security department must be determined. The primary duty of a security force is to provide proactive patrols of the maritime property or ship in order to protect life and prevent losses, respond to emergencies, and provide assistance to staff and visitors.

Security patrols may be conducted by foot patrol within the maritime buildings on docks and on ships. In outdoor parking areas, the use of vehicles such as automobiles, all-wheel drive vehicles, bicycles, or segways may be used. Small watercraft may be utilized to patrol waterways near the port facility and docks. Small watercraft may also be deployed to provide security around ships at port.

The security department should be utilized to control access to the maritime property and ships. The access control may begin at the perimeter of the maritime property and at vehicle entrances. This would include checking the Transportation Worker Identification Credentials issued by the Department of Homeland Security as well as company identification and driver's licenses based on the situation. If necessary, the security department is responsible for the inspection of vehicles entering the facility. Access control points required to be covered by security officers may also include pedestrian entrances. Escorts are often provided by a security department for visitors entering restricted areas of the port facility or onboard ships. These escorts could also be used for the transportation of money, high-value property, or confidential company information. The escorts stay on the maritime property and ship, or leave the said locations such as the case of a money escort to a banking facility. Providing security escorts to employee parking areas for employees leaving work during hours of darkness may also be a service that is provided by the security department.

Inspections of the facility for security threats, safety, and hazards that could cause losses are a function that should be performed by the security officers while on patrol. Depending on the size of the maritime property and the number of buildings and docks or the size of the ship to be patrolled, this may be a duty that would be performed by security officers on patrol.

Investigations of losses, safety issues, accidents, violations of regulations, and employee misconduct and criminal activity and possible terrorism will require the attention of investigators if there is a significant caseload based on the size and population of the maritime facility or ship. In most cases, this function would be conducted by the CSO.

Monitoring of intrusion detection and fire safety systems, security cameras, and access control points is an important function of security. The establishment of a proprietary security communications and monitoring center to dispatch security staff, answer security-related calls, monitor the security, fire safety, cameras, and access control points will require the hiring of additional security officers to perform this vital function. These positions should be staffed by trained security officers who can be rotated between patrol functions and monitoring duties.

This is critical since a trained security officer will be more effective at responding to security calls and situations arising while monitoring the security and safety systems than a person hired to only work in the communications center. It is also important to not have an individual monitor such systems for more than 2 hours. A security officer will become less effective at monitoring a security camera if the assignment lasts more than 2 hours. By having security officers working in a maritime land-based communications center, they can be rotated to the patrol function after 2 hours in the communications center.

The final function to consider is the administrative duties associated with a security department. These duties will include securing security department records, processing of internal violations such as parking tickets, preparing correspondence, monthly reports, and any other administrative duties that may be required. These positions may be in the role of secretary to the director and administrative clerks.

Based on a review of all the possible duties and functions of a security department that have been described, a final determination of what services and duties the security department will perform should be included in the position description.

LEGAL AUTHORIZATION TO PROTECT A FACILITY AND SHIP

The administrators and CSO must know the state laws relating to the policies on the apprehension of suspects at shore-based facilities. It is important to review your state laws prior to making any citizen's arrest for any criminal offense.

Authority on Ships

Security officers are authorized to enforce all property rules and regulations pertaining to security, safety, fire protection, parking, traffic, and vehicle registration at the maritime facility. The security officer also has authorization to enforce all ship security rules and regulations. This enforcement is accomplished through the writing of reports and verbal directions or commands as the situation warrants.

Security officers have the authority to stop anyone on the maritime property or onboard a ship where they are employed for the purpose of identifying such persons or determining if he or she is authorized to be in a specific area. They may also stop anyone to investigate a suspicious activity or to obtain information regarding an individual whom they believe has committed a criminal offense.

An arrest is the taking of a person into custody in order that he or she may be held to answer for or be prevented from committing a criminal offense. A citizen's arrest in most states can only be made for felonies committed in the presence of the security officer and for the safety and protection of life.

The crime codes and other laws relating to the authority of security officers of each state in which the maritime facility is located must be consulted. Each security officer should be responsible for knowing and understanding the state laws and must be training in this area.

Pedestrian Stops

Security officers should be authorized to stop anyone on the maritime facility property or on a ship with probable cause to ascertain their identity and purpose for being at the maritime facility or onboard the ship. Probable cause includes individuals acting in a suspicious manner, loitering for periods of time, and individuals seen in unauthorized areas or during times that the facility is closed to the public.

In addition to the requirements of the Department of Homeland Security Transportation Worker Identification Credentials, all staff at shore-based facilities and on ships should be required to have a photo identification card in their possession while on duty and should be required to wear it in a visible area or show it upon request.

Should an unidentifiable person be stopped and refuse to show identification, they should be escorted off of the property. Any pedestrian stop should be documented in the security officer's daily activity report. Should the stop be the result of a significant incident, an incident report should be completed.

PROFILES AND SECURITY THREATS

A review of the profile of the facility or ship to be protected is necessary when determining the size of the security department. The type operation of the maritime facility with regard to its size, hours of operation, number of employees, visitors, the type and number of small watercraft, yachts or ships as well as security threats are key elements that must be considered to determine the size of the security department.

The security threat will be based on numerous factors to include the type of property type and the type and number of small watercraft, yachts, or ships at the location. The local crime rate and previous crime and losses against the maritime facility, the yacht, and ship and where the yacht or ship will be traveling must also be evaluated to determine the current risk.

Size of the Facility and Ship

The size of the facility including the square footage of buildings, the number of floors in the buildings, and the size of a ship must be calculated when determining the number of security officers required to provide adequate protection.

Hours of Operation

Hours of operations of the maritime facility will impact the size of the security department to provide adequate security coverage. If open from 8 a.m. to 5 p.m. each day, then at night a detection system can be used, it obviously will require less security force coverage than a period of longer operations. As hours of operation lessen or expand based on the specific situation, the level of security coverage will also need to be adjusted. A ship at sea is in operation 24 hours a day.

Number of Employees–Visitors

The number of employees or a ship's crew will also have an impact on the size of the security department. The number may change by day of the week and hours of the day and need to be calculated into the security coverage for the facility. A ship's crews in most cases will remain the same when at sea.

PROPRIETARY SECURITY FORCE

A proprietary security force is one in which the security officers are employees of the maritime facility or ship. A proprietary security force may be full time, part time, or a combination of full- or part-time positions. Based on the type of position, they may qualify for full or limited company benefits such a medical coverage, insurance, vacation, and sick leave.

The advantages of a proprietary security force include control in who is hired by establishing standards and qualifications for the positions and the conducting of an extensive pre-employment background investigation. With a proprietary security force, there is more opportunity to provide professional and effective training to the staff. Other advantages are that with a proprietary security force, they will have more loyalty to the company because they are employees and because of the benefit and training packages offered. This leads to a more loyal employee and a reduction in high turnover of the security force. Long-term security officers because of their experience will be an asset to the maritime company or ship.

The disadvantages of a proprietary security force are that it takes longer to hire staff and costs more as the facility or ship must place advertisements for recruitment, conduct pre-employment background investigations, and supply uniforms and equipment. There is also the cost of a complete benefits package.

Another disadvantage is that once the security officer makes it past the probationary period, it is more difficult to terminate an officer. To do so, all actions must be documented and progressive disciplinary action must be utilized unless the offenses are serious enough to warrant immediate termination.

CONTRACT SECURITY FORCE

A contract security force is one that is made up of security officers working as employees of a licensed security or investigative firm that provides security service on a contract basis and who are not on the payroll of the firm. In most states, contract security providers must be licensed, so it is important to select a firm that meets this legal requirement.

The advantage of utilizing a contract security force is the flexibility to hire full or part time or a combination of both for whatever length of time required. The maritime company or ship utilizing the contract security officer does not need to place ads to recruit, interview, or hire the officers. It is less expensive because the licensed contractor firm pays for the benefits, training, equipment, and uniforms of the security officers. Another advantage is that contract security officers are easy to terminate. If an officer is not performing well, the security contractor can remove them from the property and replace them with another security officer.

Some of the disadvantages include a lack of loyalty by contract security officers to the firm that they are assigned as their loyalty in most cases will be with the licensed contract agency. Based on the training provided by the contract agency, it may not be at the level of a proprietary security force. There may also be a high turnover rate due to the lower pay received by contract security officers or they may be pulled from one work location to another by the contract security firm to meet various client schedule demands.

There are advantages and disadvantages to both proprietary and contract security forces. The company needs to make a determination as to which is best for their requirements and budget. A company can utilize full-time proprietary security officers, full-time contractor security officers, or a combination of both.

SECURITY DEPARTMENT UNIFORMS
AND IDENTIFICATION

Traditionally, security officers wear a uniform. A uniform is a symbol of authority and allows the security officer to be easily identified during an emergency or when assistance is required by staff or visitors to a facility or ship. The most common security uniform is slacks and a short and long sleeve police/military style shirt with a security patch, name tag, and a badge where authorized by state or local laws. This is the most common uniform for maritime shore-based operations.

During colder weather, a variety of light- and heavy-weight water-resistant jackets and coats can be utilized. Patches, name tags, and badges are also placed on the outer garment for ease of identification. Headwear is also a part of the security uniform and can be a more formal eight-point cap, trooper hat, or ball cap style with a badge or security insignia placed on the front of the headwear.

A softer uniform image may be selected rather than a traditional security uniform. It often consists of a jacket, tie, and slacks that may have a security patch attached with a name tag. Where permitted by law, a security badge may be displayed on the jacket using a pocket holder. In warmer season or climates, the softer uniform may be slacks with a shirt and tie or a polo-type shirt with security patches, name tags, and badges. The security attire may be business dress or business casual rather than a distinctive uniform. If this type of clothing is utilized, a name tag and a security badge in a pocket holder should be utilized for easy identification of a security officer.

Onboard a ship, security officers should wear a less formal tactical security uniform for comfort and functionality. On cruise ships, security officers in most cases will have a more formal appearance.

Just as the security uniform provides a symbol, so does security department identification. Badges, where authorized by state and local law, are a universally recognized symbol of authority. Shoulder patches also add to the authority of the security officer and identify the company or contract agency with whom they are employed. The most important aspect of security identification is a photo identification card to be worn on the uniform or carried in a case. This will provide a positive identification of the security officer where they work.

Security uniforms and identification allow the security officer to be identified as an authority figure, but uniforms and identification alone do not provide the security officer with such authority. The authority must come from legal codes that apply to the security officer depending on the state in which they operate. The authority also comes from the company for which they are employed. This legitimacy must also be based on the proper use of such authority.

STAFF AND VISITOR IDENTIFICATION

In addition to the Transportation Worker Identification Credentials (TWICs) (see Figure 5.1), all staff should be issued photo marina, maritime facility, or ship identification cards, and they should be worn in plain view when at work. This will allow for immediate identification of authorized individuals in areas of the property that are restricted and are not open to the public. The wearing of the photo identification by staff also allows visitors to identify staff members if they need assistance or have questions. The photo identification cards should also be utilized for access control. When using proximity card readers on property doors, the photo identification cards can also be a proximity card used to operate the access control units on the doors. The same card can also be used for timekeeping.

The wearing of photo identification by staff can also be of value in the prevention of crime. As staff walk around the property they will be identified by potential perpetrators that could deter criminal activity.

Visitor identification should be utilized for visitors to the property who will be accessing restricted areas not open to the public. This will allow staff and security to identify authorized visitors to these areas and provide documentation of the visitor arrival and departure as the visitor identification is signed out to the visitor and then returned by the visitor.

The computer-based photo identification system, card access system, and visitor identification should be administered by the

FIGURE 5.1   Transportation Worker Identification Credential (TWIC). (Photograph by Daniel J. Benny.)

security department. Strict inventory control must be established for all staff and visitor identification cards that are issued.

SECURITY DEPARTMENT PROTECTIVE EQUIPMENT

Where authorized by the federal law, state law, and international and maritime law when onboard a ship protective equipment may be considered for the security department. The type of protective equipment utilized will be based on the threat level, location, and mission of the security department and may range from handcuffs to the carrying of firearms. Many states require specialized training before being authorized to carry various types of protective equipment. In Pennsylvania, for example, security officers who carry a baton or firearm must complete what is known as the Lethal Weapons Act 235 Course. To attend the 40-hour course, the student must submit to a criminal background check and medical and psychology evaluations. The 40-hour course covers the legal aspects of carrying a weapon, the authority of a security officer, use of force considerations, and the Pennsylvania Crimes Code. Students must pass a written test and qualify on the firing range to become certified under the Lethal Weapons Act. It is important to know the requirements with regard to carrying a weapon in the state in which security officers are operating to ensure compliance with the laws of the state.

Handcuffs are an important tool should the security officer be required to make a citizen's arrest during the performance of his or her duties. Handcuffs provide a means to secure an individual who becomes violent either before or after a citizen's arrest. The use of handcuffs in such situations provides safety to the security officer and the public. Handcuffs should be of good quality and have the capability of being doubled-locked. The double-locking mechanism prevents the handcuff from being tightened on the suspect by accident or by the suspect to then claim an injury from their use.

Oleoresin Capsicum or OC Spray is a lachrymatory irritant agent that can be carried by security officers. It provides a nonlethal method of self-defense for the security officer and is very effective in most situations. Security officers should be certified by the manufacturer of the Oleoresin Capsicum product to ensure proper use and for liability purposes.

Batons have been carried by security and police officers for over a 100 years and they can be used as both a defensive and an offensive protective tool. When used offensively, they are considered a deadly weapon. Batons come in various styles to include the traditional striate baton, the collapsible ASP baton, and the PR-24 full-size or collapsible model (Figure 5.2). Certification should be obtained from the manufacturer of the particular baton that is carried for proper use and liability protection.

FIGURE 5.2 APR-24 baton and ASP baton. (Photograph by Daniel J. Benny.)

Firearms may be carried by the security department based on the legal requirements of the state for shore-based facilities. The threat and mission of the security department at a particular site must also be considered. If a security officer carries a firearm they must be equipped with alternate means of protective equipment such as a baton and Oleoresin Capsicum. This provides the security officer with a nonlethal response option if use of deadly force would not be authorized based on the situation.

A revolver or semiautomatic firearm may be carried (Figures 5.3 and 5.4). In some situations, security officers may also carry a shotgun (Figure 5.5). In addition to state legal requirements for qualification and certification to carry a firearm, security officers should be trained and qualified with the weapons and ammunition they carry at least once a year. Many security departments require such training and qualification at least twice and up to four times a year.

Security officers who carry this protective equipment must be trained with the use of force continuum and the company use of force policy.

USE OF FORCE OPTIONS

- Security Officer Presence—No force is used. Considered the best way to resolve a situation. The mere presence of a security officer works to deter crime or diffuse a situation.

FIGURE 5.3 Sig Sauer 9-mm model 228 and Sig Sauer 40 Cal. model 229 with a laser sight are examples of semiautomatic pistols used by the Naval Criminal Investigative Service, the U.S. Coast Guard, and private security. (Photograph by Daniel J. Benny.)

- Security officers' attitudes are professional and nonthreatening.
- Verbalization —Force is nonphysical.
  - Security officers issue calm, nonthreatening commands, such as "Let me see your identification."
  - Security officers may increase their volume and shorten commands in an attempt to gain compliance. Short commands might include "Stop," or "Don't move."
- Empty-Hand Control—Security officers use bodily force to gain control of a situation.
  - *Soft technique.* Security officers use grabs, holds, and joint locks to restrain an individual.
  - *Hard technique.* Security officers use punches and kicks to restrain an individual.

FIGURE 5.4 Smith & Wesson .44 Magnum and various Colt .38 and .32 Cal. revolvers that have been used by security over the years. (Photograph by Daniel J. Benny.)

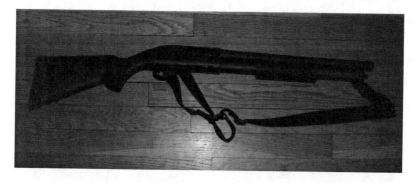

FIGURE 5.5 Remington 870 12-Gauge Tactical Shotgun. (Photograph by Daniel J. Benny.)

- Less-Lethal Methods—Security officers use less-lethal technologies to gain control of a situation.
  - *Blunt impact.* Security officers may use a baton to immobilize a combative person.
  - *Chemical.* Security officers may use chemical sprays or projectiles embedded with chemicals to restrain an individual.
- Lethal Force—Security officers may use lethal weapons to gain control of a situation. These should only be used if a suspect poses a serious threat to the security officer or another individual.
- Security officers can use deadly weapons such as firearms or a baton, striking a vital area of the body (head, neck, kidney, or groin) to stop an individual's actions.

SECURITY DEPARTMENT VEHICLES

A security department may maintain and operate patrol vehicles for use at the shore-based maritime property for patrolling docks, parking areas, and roadways. Based on the size of the property and climate conditions, an automobile may be used or a four-wheel drive vehicle may be selected.

The vehicles should be visibly marked as in accordance with state law (see Figure 5.6).

FIGURE 5.6 The U.S. Navy security patrol vehicle at Ship Parts Control Center, Mechanicsburg, Pennsylvania. (Photograph by Daniel J. Benny.)

Emergency Vehicle Lighting

Emergency lighting, where permitted by state law, should be utilized when stopping on roadways or parking areas during vehicle inquiries. Emergency lighting may also be used when responding to calls on the property, when conducting traffic control or for increased visibility during routine patrol.

SECURITY DEPARTMENT COMMUNICATIONS

Several means of communications should be available to the security department to ensure immediate and effective communications during both routine and emergency situations. These should include portable two-way radios and mobile two-way radios if there are security vehicles on the property (see Figure 5.7). Emergency call boxes are recommended both inside the building and at outside parking and walkway areas that can be used by security, staff, or visitors in case of emergency. The use of mobile telephones by security officers is also recommended for emergency communications. A method to make a public announcement is recommended in the event of an emergency, such as an active shooter on the cultural property and to aid in evacuations.

FIGURE 5.7   Security force communications, telephone, mobile phones, and security radios. (Photograph by Daniel J. Benny.)

When using any form of communications, members of the security department are expected to communicate in a professional and service-oriented manner. When using two-way radios, Federal Communications Commission (FCC) guidelines must be adhered to. At no time while talking on any type of communications equipment should members of the security department utilize CB or other types of slang or jargon, nor should profanity be used on the communications system.

SECURITY DEPARTMENT REPORTS

In order to document the incidents, complaints, and activities in which the security department becomes involved, various reports will be required. All reports should be written on a computer if possible. The use of a type written or printed in ink using block letters is acceptable.

Completed security department reports are to be considered legal documents as they may be utilized in criminal, civil, governmental, or cultural property proceedings. Reports and the information contained in them must be protected.

Incident/Complaint Reports

The Incident/Complaint Report form should be utilized to document all important incidents that occur on the property. The type of incidents that should be reported include criminal activity, accidents, vehicle accidents, medical emergencies, fire or safety emergencies, hazmat spills, reports of suspicious activity, and any other incident or activity in which any member of the security department becomes involved or believed is worth documenting. If in doubt, the security officer should complete an Incident/Complaint Report.

Each Incident/Complaint Report should be numbered. As an example beginning with the year, the month, and numerical report number for the calendar year. Example:

January 12, 2016, the date of the first report of the year would read as follows: 01-12-2016-001.

January 13, 2016, the date of the second report would read as follows: 01-13-2016-002.

Daily Activity Reports

All security officers should complete a Daily Activity Report during their shift. This report will be utilized to document their time of arrival and departure, inspection of the patrol vehicle, where applicable, and to document routine activities. Routine activities include building and door unlocking and locking, escorts, and checking of buildings in various areas of the cultural property. The Daily Activity Report should also show the initial response to an incident or complaint and reference the Incident/Complaint Report number. The Daily Activity Report should be maintained in a file in the security office.

A Security Department Training Record needs to be maintained by the CSO for all security staff and will be used to document the training of all security department members.

PROTECTION OF SECURITY DEPARTMENT INFORMATION

All information, whether received orally or in written form, pertaining to security department incidents or investigations being conducted is confidential information. Such information should only be disseminated to authorized individuals on a need to know basis.

Information should not be released to individuals not associated with the facility or ship unless approved by the CSO. Any requests for information from members of the media will be referred to the CSO.

All sensitive security documents must be secured in a locked security container when not being used. This includes both final and draft copies of incident reports, statements, investigative notes, safety and security reports, and audits and inspections. Sensitive documents that are no longer needed will be shredded prior to placing them in removal containers.

ETHICS AND CONDUCT

Ethics

All security department personnel are expected to maintain the highest professional and moral standards. The quality of a professional security department ultimately depends upon the willingness of the practitioners to observe special standards of conduct and to manifest good faith in professional relationships.

The following Professional Code of Ethics, as established by ASIS International, will distinguish the professional from the nonprofessional.

AMERICAN SOCIETY FOR INDUSTRIAL
SECURITY INTERNATIONAL

Professional Code of Ethics

I. *Perform professional duties in accordance with the laws and highest moral principles.*

II. *Observe the precepts of truthfulness, honesty, and integrity.*

III. *Be faithful and diligent in discharging professional responsibilities.*

IV. *Be competent in discharging professional responsibilities.*

V. *Do not maliciously injure the professional reputation of colleagues.*

SECURITY DEPARTMENT TRAINING

One of the most important aspects in the management of a security department is to ensure that the security officers are effectively trained to meet any state regulatory requirements as well as security industry standards of training. Such training will promote professionalism within the security force and reduce the liability risk. Security force training can be accomplished by on-the-job experience and training and through the use of various formal education methods.

On-the-job experience and training comprises a structured and documented approach in instructing the new security officer with regard to his or her day-to-day duties as a security officer. Each new security officer should be assigned to a mentor. The mentor may be a supervisor, lead officer, or training officer who will guide the new officer through their daily activities, providing instruction on how to perform their duties. As each new task is learned, it should be documented in a written training record for each security officer.

As the security officer accumulates time in the profession and the various security assignments, he or she will gain knowledge and proficiency in his or her profession. Other on-the-job educational tools may include having the security officer take part in organizational meetings and committees to expand his or her professional knowledge. This may include being part of a security and safety committee or meetings related to special events that might be scheduled.

In addition to on-the-job training, more formal educational methods should also be applied. This may include company assistance for the security officer to obtain a college degree in security or criminal justice. In-service training can also be used, where the security officer is provided with information in a classroom environment covering security procedures, report writing, patrol methods, or court testament. In-service training can also be used to provide the security officer with various certifications, such as first aid and CPR, handcuff, OC or baton certification.

Another option for education is to have the security officer take part in self-study by online proprietary training or a website offering free training such as the Homeland Security Federal Emergency Management Agency Academy. Time for such online training can be provided during the work schedule or it can be accomplished off duty. Directed reading is another source of education where articles or documents related to security are made available in the security office in which the security officers are required to read and sign off on the document that has been read.

In order to ensure that the security department is professionally trained, a security training program needs to be established and mandatory training needs to be provided to all security officers. All state regulatory training requirements, where applicable, must all be completed. It is important that all training completed by each security officer be documented in the security officer's training file. This will allow for the tracking of the training to ensure that it has been completed as such documentation is required by regulatory agencies or can be related to liability issues.

PROFESSIONAL SECURITY CERTIFICATIONS

Professional security certifications can be obtained and are of value to those in the security profession. As discussed previously, ASIS International has developed several professional security certifications for individuals working in security supervision and management. They also have two certifications for nonmanagement security professionals. The Professional Certified Investigator (PCI) was established for the security investigator or private investigators. Upon successful completion of the examination that covers all aspects of security and private investigation to include investigative methods, legal considerations, and interview methods, the designation of PCI is bestowed.

The Physical Security Professional (PSP) designation is designed for those in security who are responsible for the physical security at a marina or on a ship. The examination covers intrusion detection systems, barriers, security cameras, locks, and access controls. Upon successful completion of the examination, the designation of PSP is bestowed.

SECURITY PATROLS

The primary duty of a security officer is to patrol the maritime property and ships. The purpose of the patrol function is to have the security officer at the right place at the right time to prevent losses due to criminal activity, safety concerns, and during an emergency. A uniformed security also provides for a deterrent and symbol of authority as they patrol the property.

Foot patrol is used to patrol inside of a structure and on a ship. It allows for close observation of the property and positive interaction with the property staff, ship's crew, and visitors. In large structures, small battery-operated security vehicle may be deployed for fast response especially if there is a need to transport emergency equipment or individuals. Foot patrol is also utilized on the exterior of properties to patrol walkways, docks, parking areas, and other segments of the property.

Properties with expansive parking areas, dock facilities, roadways, and open areas cannot be patrolled effectively by a security officer on foot, especially during periods of cold and inclement weather. In these situations, a means of patrol needs to be provided that will allow the security officer to cover large areas in a timely manner during both routine patrol and in response to service calls and emergencies.

The most common means of patrol in this situation would be a motor vehicle assigned to the security department that is clearly marked as a security vehicle. It may be an automobile or an all-wheel vehicle. This will be based on the roadways and layout of the property as well as the local climate. A property that is located in an area that receives snowfall should consider the use of an all-wheel drive security vehicle to ensure that security patrols can be accomplished in inclement weather or where there is a need for off-road capabilities.

During warm weather, bicycles may be considered as patrol vehicles. They allow for fast response and are a valuable public relations tool as it promoted more interaction with staff and visitor to the property.

To provide additional security at marinas and port facilities, the security department may utilize small watercraft as security patrol boats to protect waterways, docks, yachts, and ships in the area (see Figure 5.8).

All security patrols must be conducted in a random manner so that patterns and predictability cannot be established. If the security patrol becomes predictable, then individuals with the intent of taking part in criminal activity to include industrial espionage be it property staff, professional criminals, or terrorist can plan their activity as not to be discovered by security patrols. If patterns are established by the security officer on patrol, the officer can become complacent and less

FIGURE 5.8   The author's 17-foot Boston Whaler, a watercraft often used for security patrols around the dock areas of a marina or port. (Photograph by Daniel J. Benny.)

observant of his or her surroundings thus reducing the effectiveness of the security patrol.

To reduce predictability, the security officer on patrol should use the concept of backtracking. An example of this would be a security walk through an area, then turning around and walking back through the same area or walking up a flight of stairs, turning around, and walking back down again.

There are two categories of patrol: supervised and unsupervised. Supervised patrol is one that is monitored and tracked by the use of proximity readers placed throughout a marina, port, or ship that the security officer must activate as he or she makes a set number of security rounds during his or her patrol schedule. This can also be accomplished by having the security officer communicate with the central station at set points during the patrol route.

The goal of this method is to document that the security officer did in fact cover all areas of the property and if monitored live to be alerted if the security officer does not scan the reader. This provides safety for the officer in the event that there is a security incident taking place or the security has an accident or medical emergency. This method of supervised patrol is recommended when a security officer is conducting a patrol during times when the property is closed or when patrolling remote areas of a property.

During hours when the maritime property is open to the public, a supervised patrol is not recommended. During those periods of time, the security officer should use unsupervised patrol meaning that the security officer does not need to check in at specified points on a patrol route. For the officers' safety, they should be required to check in by radio at predetermined times during their patrolling schedule. The reason a supervised method of patrol is not recommended when the property is open is that the security officer will be more concerned in documenting the supervised patrol that he or she may not be as effective in interacting with visitors and staff.

A security officer patrol awareness color code can be used to illustrate the proper attentiveness of a security officer during the course of his or her assigned shift.

White: This is when the security officer is unaware of his or her surroundings. The security officer is thinking of personal matters rather than being alert during patrol. A security officer on patrol in the white awareness mode is not doing his or her job and is placing himself or herself, visitors, and staff at risk.

Green: This is the awareness color code for normal patrol. A security officer can and should be at this level of awareness during the entire patrol. In fact it is the level that everyone should be at when out and about in public places. At this level, the security officer will use all of his or her senses. Vision is the number one sensor where the security officer can see all potential and actual threats. Hearing is the second most important sense. A security officer may hear an alarm going off, a call for help, or a transmission on the security radio. The security may also hear someone approaching in low visibility. Smell is also an important sensor in the security profession. A security officer may smell smoke or a natural gas leak and be able to prevent a serious incident. If a suspicious person approached the security officer and the person approaching security is intoxicated or has been smoking marijuana the security may be able to smell it and be alert to an individual who may not be in his or her normal state of mind. The final sense is that of touch. This may be of value to the security officer to determine if equipment is overheating or if a vehicle found on the property parking areas was recently driven by the engine heat on the hood of the vehicle.

Yellow: This is the level when the security officer is alerted to something unusual, which is based on one of the officer's senses. The security officer becomes alert and begins to evaluate the situation and make a determination if it needs further investigation or if it is okay to return to normal patrol awareness or the green mode.

Red: This is the full-reaction mode where the security officer must respond to protect himself, others, or the facility. If the security officer is alert, he or she should never be surprised and go from green to red mode. With that said, no one is perfect and it can happen.

It is critical that the security officer knows his or her patrol area. This means that the security officer should have a working knowledge of the physical layout of the site or ship to include the interior of all building and the exterior property. The security officer needs to know what is normal based on the time of day and day of the week. This will allow him or her discern what is not normal and alert him or her to suspicious criminal activity or a safety hazard. The security officer should also be aware of any special activity occurring during his or her patrol schedule such as special events, construction, or an area of the property that may be temporarily closed to the public.

When conducting a patrol, the security officer should utilize the concepts of loss prevention and assets protection with the goal of prevention losses due to criminal activity and safety hazards. The patrol should be highly visible so that visitors and staff see the uniformed security officers frequently. This will also mean that any potential perpetrator will also see the security officers and it may deter unwanted activity.

APPREHENSION AND ARREST

Members of the security department are not police officers and generally will not make apprehensions and arrests. They should only act in accordance with the state law and company policy at shore-based maritime facilities and international and maritime law when at sea. Apprehensions and arrests may only be conducted should the security officer witness the commission of a felony. Security officers may also make an apprehension of a violent person in order to protect themselves or another person from bodily harm.

BIBLIOGRAPHY

Fischer, R. J., & Green, G. (2012). *Introduction to security* (9th ed). Burlington, MA: Elseivier.

International Maritime Organization. (2012). *Guide to maritime security and the ISPS code*. London, UK: Author.

Kovacich, G. L., & Halibozek, E. P. (2004). *The manager's handbook for corporate security*. New York: Butterworth-Heinemann.

United States Coast Guard. (2014.) United States Counter Piracy and Maritime Security Action Plan. Washington, DC: U.S. Government Printing Office.

CHAPTER 6

Marina Security

A marina is a maritime docking and mooring facility primarily used for small watercraft such as powerboats, sailboats, and yachts. A marina may be located on a lake, river, or intracoastal waterway. The marina may also be located at sea.

These havens for the maritime community may provide a variety of maritime services such as refueling, washing, and repair facilities. The marina may also sell new or preowner watercraft and boat engines. Boat ramps for accessing the water by boats that are trailered may also be provided. In addition to docking and mooring services, the marina often provides trailer and boat storage on the property. Outdoor or indoor storage of watercraft is a service that is frequently provided (Figure 6.1).

The marina may have non-boat services such as vehicle parking lots, picnic areas, a clubhouse, restaurants, and shops. These services can be a fee-based marina operation or they could be contracted out with the marina leasing the space for the services to an outside vendor.

MARINA SECURITY PLANS

To have an effective security program, the marina needs to establish a written marina security plan. The marina security plan is based on the threat assessment conducted by the facility. This will include the history of past criminal incidents and losses as well as potential threats in the future as described in Chapter 2 of this book.

The location of the marina and the proximity of public safety support such as the U.S. Coast Guard and local police, fire, and emergency medical services will factor into the threat assessment.

There are several principles that must be considered when conducting a threat assessment of a marina. These include protection of individuals on the property, boathouses, seaplane aircraft, fuel storage, office areas, watercraft, and other tenants that may be situated at the marina.

FIGURE 6.1   Long Level Marina, Wrightsville, Pennsylvania. (Photograph by Daniel J. Benny.)

The threat assessment, in addition to traditional criminal activity, must also take into account the risk of terrorism and the possibility of watercraft being used as a weapon.

Once the threat or risk has been identified, the next step is to determine what is required to protect the marina from those risks. This is accomplished by conducting an examination of the risk severity and probability of occurrence as follows:

Threat: (risk of threat = severity of threat × probability of occurrence).

The security measures should be implemented in order to reduce the threat. A review of the security measures and plans should then be made and any changes made as needed.

After conducting the threat assessment, the next step is the development of a written marina security plan that details all of the security measures that are implemented. The marina should designate an individual to be the marina security coordinator and a marina security committee should be established. This person should take the lead in the development of the marina security plan with the assistance of the marina security committee. The individual may be the marina manager or owner depending on the organizational structure of a marina. It can be anyone the marina designates; the important factor is that the appointment be made to ensure the development and continued operation of an effective marina security plan. The committee should be made up of representatives of the marina, such as owners/management, tenants, boat owners, the local police chief, local fire chief, the U.S. Coast Guard and/or the state waterway law enforcement agency.

The written marina security plan needs to cover all security aspects of the maritime facility, which includes the protection of the perimeter of the marina, access on the property, roadways, fueling area, docks, and watercraft. The marina security plan should begin with a cover page identifying the marina name. This is followed by a table of contents. The next section would be the introduction where the purpose of the marina security plan is stated to show the maritime community that the security of the marina is important.

The fact that a security coordinator and the security committee have been established should be addressed next with a listing of the titles of who will make up that committee. A list of important contacts should be next in this section of the security plan. It should include the marina manager, and/or owner, the security coordinator, and may also include the members of the security committee.

The next area of the marina security plan would be the communications section. This will include all the nonemergency and emergency phone numbers such as the manager, security coordinator, tenants, local police, fire, and emergency agencies, and the U.S. Coast Guard. This part of the plan should also include the U.S. Coast Guard America's Waterway Watch program.

The subsequent section of the marina security plan should provide physical information on the marina facility. This would include the number of docks (including their length), the number of watercraft or seaplanes based at the facility, and special use of watercraft such as by law enforcement, emergency medical, firefighting, water rescue, or U.S. Coast Guard Auxiliary.

Any possible terrorist targets in the area of the marina that could be attacked by the use of the local waterways and boats from the marina should be listed in this section of the security plan. This could include military facilities, national landmarks, government buildings, power plants, dams, power lines, pipelines, larger sports venues, or large population areas.

Other areas of security that need to be addressed in this part of the plan would include access control onto the facility by land and around the buildings, dock, and watercraft. Security lighting, marina information, and security signage should also be addressed in the security plan.

A marina layout or sketch showing the perimeter boundary, roadways, buildings, ramps, and docks should be placed in the security plan. This will allow for a visual reference of the marina.

The next part of the security plan should cover security and law enforcement support of the marina. The security may be provided by staff as a collateral duty. The security may also be professional proprietary security officers hired by the marina or contracted through a licensed contact security agency. A description of the law enforcement coverage should also be listed. In most cases, this would include drive-bys during the day or evening hours and response to emergencies.

The final area of the marina security plan should cover the identification of suspicious activity that may be observed at the marina that would warrant reporting. The reporting protocols should be addressed in this area. The reporting and response to emergency situations will be the final topic addressed in this area of the marina security plan.

The marina security plan is not a legal requirement, so the marina can write into the plan what that facility feels is important to security at that location. For liability reasons and professional creditability, never write anything in the marina security plan that you are not doing or cannot accomplish.

The marina security plan must be updated whenever there is a change to the security program. The plan should be reviewed at least once a year to ensure that it is current and the review and updating if required should be documented in writing.

The following sample marina security plan can be used as a template in the development of a marina security plan. Each plan will vary in complexity based on the size of the facility and the vehicle and watercraft activities at the marina and surrounding areas.

SAMPLE

Marina Security Plan

Marina Name
Town and State

TABLE OF CONTENTS

C. Access Control
D. Intrusion Detection Systems
E. Boathouses
F. Watercraft
G. Lighting
H. Signage
I. Fueling
J. Marina Layout Sketch (Layout/Location)
K. Boating School Operations (If Any)
L. Restricted Areas
M. Doors, Windows, and Utility Ports on Building
N. Office and Cash-Handling Security
IV. Security and Law Enforcement Support
    A. USCG America's Waterway Watch Program
    B. Routine Patrols
V. Incident Reporting/Emergency Response
    A. Suspicious Activity
    B. Criminal Activity, Bomb Threats, Terrorism, or Other Emergency

PART I INTRODUCTION

A. PURPOSE

The goal of this marina security plan is to provide an overview of the security measures that have been established for the marina in order to ensure the security and safety of the boat owners, watercraft, tenants, and staff. The security plan will provide the procedures to use in an emergency, security, or safety situation and protocol to report suspicious behavior.

B. MARINA SECURITY COORDINATOR AND COMMITTEE

A marina security coordinator has been named and a marina security committee has been established consisting of the marina manager, chief of police, fire chief, and a watercraft owner. The committee will meet annually to review security at the marina and establish and update security procedures as needed.

C. POINTS OF CONTACT

The Marina Manager/Security Coordinator point of contact is _____ _____, and can be contacted at _____ during working hours and _____ after hours.

PART II COMMUNICATIONS

A. CONTACT INFORMATION

The contact information is posted in marina office.

MARINA EMERGENCY CONTACT INFORMATION

AGENCY	CONTACT	TELEPHONE	ALTERNATE #
Manager/Security		911	
Fire Department Emergency Medical Service Police			
Police Department Nonemergency			
The U.S. Coast Guard			
The U.S. Coast Guard Auxiliary			

America's
  Waterway Watch
  Program
	Department of
	Homeland Security,
	U.S. Coast Guard
		877-24WATCH	

B. Boat Owners/Tenants

MARINA BOAT OWNERS AND TENANTS

Marina Office: _____

ADDRESS: _____

TELEPHONE: _____

NAME OF WATERCRAFT OR SEAPLANE OWNER/ TENANT	TELEPHONE	TYPE BOAT OR SEAPLANE	BOAT NUMBER OR SEAPLANE "N" NUMBER	DOCK#

PART III MARINA PHYSICAL SECURITY

A. GENERAL INFORMATION

_____ marina has _____ docks.
There are _____ watercraft and/or seaplanes based at the marina.

ACTIVITIES AT THE MARINA INCLUDE THE FOLLOWING:

Boat instruction:	USCG Auxiliary:
Boat rental:	Air ambulance:
Charter service:	Boat repair:
Law enforcement:	Boat sales:

Military Bases within 30 nm? _____.

Power Plants within 30 nm? _____.

Highly Populated Areas (50,000+) within 30 nm?_____.

B. LANDSCAPING AND GROUNDS

Building entrances should be accentuated through landscaping and/or paving features.

All public entrances should be clearly defined by walkways and signage.

Landscape should be maintained to provide good visibility around buildings.

Vegetation should be trimmed to eliminate potential hiding places on the marina property.

Ensure that trees or other landscape features do not provide access to the roof or other upper levels of the buildings or over and security fencing on the marina property.

Trees and vegetation should be kept trimmed to prevent from interfering with lighting.

Ensure that trash dumpsters and trash enclosures do not create blind spots or hiding areas.

Ensure that the marina land perimeter is clearly defined by landscaping or fencing.

C. ACCESS CONTROL

The marina should have chain link perimeter security fencing.

The land side of the perimeter of the marina should be completely fenced.

Vehicle access must be controlled or restricted by fencing, gates, use of security signs, access control, and security cameras.

Maintenance of roads that provide access to the waterway side area must be controlled at all times.

Law enforcement and emergency personnel should be provided a key or access code to all locked gates at the marina.

Security camera surveillance should be installed at the marina and monitored.

Pedestrian access must be controlled to dock areas.

Photo-badge ID system should be in use for all staff.

Sign-in/Sign-out procedures should be in place for all transients (vendors, contractors, etc.) entering the dock area.

D. Intrusion Detection Systems

An intrusion detection system should be utilized to protect buildings.

The intrusion detection system should be certified by Underwriters Laboratory.

The intrusion detection system should be tested daily.

The intrusion detection system should report to a contract central station or proprietary central station.

Automatic backup power supply that activates during power failures should be installed.

The intrusion detection system should employ antitamper technology.

E. Boathouses

The marina has _____ conventional boathouse with a total capacity of _____ watercraft.

Each boathouse should be equipped with padlocks on pedestrian doors and a locking system for the main doors.

It should be the policy of this marina to keep boathouse doors shut and locked when tenants are not present and watercraft are in the boathouse.

Control vehicle and pedestrian traffic to boathouses.

F. Watercraft

All watercraft owners should be encouraged to practice good security with regard to their boats.

Lock or otherwise secure watercraft engines.

Cabin windows should be covered to prevent thieves from observing electronics and other content.

G. Lighting

Boathouses, fueling areas, and all key access areas must be well lighted from dusk to dawn.

Proper lighting levels should be maintained at all door and window openings during hours of darkness.

Develop a schedule for maintenance inspections to ensure that lights are in good working order at all times.

H. Signage

Restrictive signs should be posted at vehicular and pedestrian access points to control access.

Clear signage related to perimeter, building entry, and visitor parking need to be displayed.

No trespassing and restricted area signs should be posted along the perimeter fencing and at restricted areas.

I. Fueling

Fueling pumps must be locked when the marina is unattended.

If 24-hour self-fueling is allowed at this marina, then access control cards or keys should be issued to the authorized individuals.

The fuel storage should not be accessible from exterior perimeter public roads.

The fueling area should be secured by fencing, security cameras, and locked when not in use or after operating hours of the marina.

Vehicle parking areas must be separated from the fueling areas.

J. Marina Layout Sketch (Layout/Location)

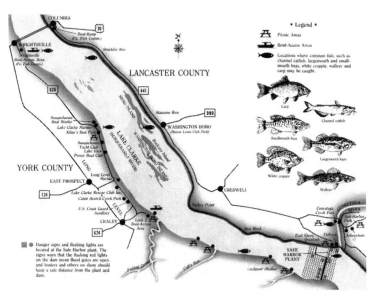

(Sample Location Diagram: Long Level Marina, Pennsylvania)

K. BOAT SCHOOL OPERATIONS

All boating school staff should be trained annually in security awareness.

The identity of individuals renting should be validated by checking a government-issued photo IDs.

Established positive identification of any student.

L. RESTRICTED AREAS

Barriers such as fences and locked gates should be utilized to prevent unauthorized vehicles from entering.

Restricted areas include boathouses, dock and watercraft dry storage, and fueling and fuel storage areas.

Restricted areas must be properly posted to keep out unauthorized individuals.

Signage should be prominently displayed near areas of public access warning against tampering with watercraft.

The restricted area should be fully secured with fencing.

The fence and gates must always be in good repair.

The security fence should be at least 7 feet in height with a 1-foot top guard facing outward at a 45-degree angle.

Adequate security lighting needs to be utilized during the hours of darkness.

All gates should be secured with high-security padlocks.

Security seals should be used on all locked gates in the restricted areas.

M. DOORS, WINDOWS, AND UTILITY PORTS ON BUILDINGS

Doors

All exterior doors should be made of metal or solid core wood design.

Sliding glass doors need to be equipped with supplemental pin locks and antilift devices.

Exposed hinges need to have nonremovable pins.

High-security deadbolt locks should be used.

The lock needs to be designed, or the doorframe constructed, so that the door cannot be open by force by spreading the frame.

Key control of the doors is vital to the security of the structure.

Doors with panic hardware must be properly secured to prevent opening and activation from the exterior.

Windows

Unused windows should be permanently sealed.

Accessible windows should be protected by burglary-resistant glazing, security film, heavy screen, or bars wherever possible.

Window locks need to be designed so that they cannot be defeated by merely breaking the glass.

Horizontal sliding windows need to be equipped with secondary locks and antilift devices.

Utility Ports

Skylights should be protected by bars or polycarbonate glazing or an intrusion detection system.

Roof hatches must be securely locked.

Ports for ventilators or air conditioning ducts and fan openings must be adequately protected with bars or wire mesh.

Roof ladders and other roof access points must be removed or secured against unauthorized use.

Roll-up and sliding doors should be properly mounted and secured with high-quality locks.

Utility rooms both inside and outside buildings need to be properly secured.

N. OFFICE AND CASH-HANDLING SECURITY

Restrict office keys to those who actually need them.

Keep strict key control of the office keys issued and up-to-date records of the disbursement of all office keys.

Prohibit duplication of office keys except for those that are specifically ordered in writing.

Mark "Do not duplicate" on all keys to prevent legitimate locksmiths from making copies without your knowledge.

Procedures need to be in place for the collection of keys from terminated employees.

All keys need to be stored in a secure wall cabinet.

Secure all office equipment such as computers with some type of locking device.

Keep a record showing issuance and return of every key, including name of person, date, and time.

Use telephone locks to prevent unauthorized phone usage when offices are unattended.

Provide secure areas for employees to store their personal property.

Record all equipment serial numbers and file them in a safe place.

Have a paper shredder and shred sensitive documents before discarding them.

Lock briefcases and bags containing important materials in a safe place when not in use.

Insist on proper identification from all vendors and repair persons who enter the marina facility.

Keep desk clear of important papers everywhere when the office is closed.

Frequently change the combination to the safe.

Emergency phone numbers should be posted near all phones.

Cash Handling

Cash registers and cash drawers need to be located beyond the reach of customers.

Make regular bank deposits or utilize an armored transport service to avoid keeping large sums of money in the office when closed.

Train employees in proper cash-handling procedures.

Employees need to be trained in proper procedures to follow during and after a robbery.

Installed panic/robbery alarm stations that may be used by employees during robberies or emergency situations.

Leave cash registers and cash drawers empty and open after working hours.

PART IV SECURITY AND LAW ENFORCEMENT SUPPORT

A. USCG America's Waterway Watch Program

The marina should use the watch program.

America's Waterway Watch signs should be posted at strategic locations.

Local police need to be aware of the America's Waterway Watch program.

B. Routine Patrols

Law enforcement agency should provide routine patrols.

Law enforcement personnel should be trained on buildings, locations, docks, and operations procedures.

Proprietary or contract security patrols should be considered to provide security of the marina.

PART V INCIDENT REPORTING/EMERGENCY RESPONSE

A. Suspicious Activity

Notify: Manager, America's Waterway Watch Program

B. Criminal Activity, Bomb Threats, Terrorism, or Other Emergency

Call 911 and initiate emergency response plan.

Restrict site access until it is secured by public safety staff.

Notify manager/security coordinator, tenants, key staff.

SIGNATURE PAGE

Signed this _____ day of _____, 2015

_____
Marina Manager

_____
Mailing Address

_____
City/State/Zip

_____
Telephone

Marina Security Awareness Program

Security awareness is the first line of defense in the protection of the marina. To be effective, the entire maritime community must be involved. Adoption of the U.S. Coast Guard America's Waterway Watch program is recommended. The goals of the U.S. Coast Guard America's Waterway Watch program are to enhance security in the maritime community and to aid in the prevention and reduction of crime in the maritime community. The U.S. Coast Guard America's Waterway Watch program encompasses two concepts related to physical security and security awareness. As it relates to physical security, the program recommends and encourages the maritime community to utilize physical security practices to prevent and reduce crime in securing boats and marinas.

The security awareness aspect of the program focuses on making marina owners and employees, as well as boat owners and seaplane pilots, aware of their surroundings. This includes being aware as to what is considered normal activity at the marina and surrounding maritime environment and what is not.

To involve the maritime community, hold periodic security awareness meetings and training programs for staff and boat owners docked at the facility. Promote security by the use of the U.S. Coast Guard America's Waterway Watch program signs and information (see Figures 6.2 and 6.3).

FIGURE 6.2 The U.S. Coast Guard America's Waterway Watch program sign. (Photograph by Daniel J. Benny.)

FIGURE 6.3 The U.S. Coast Guard America's Waterway Watch program information pass outs. (Photograph by Daniel J. Benny.)

If the marina has a website, that would be an excellent location to address security awareness. It can also be used to link to other maritime security-related websites.

Physical Security for the Marina

Marina Perimeter Security

The perimeter security of the marina begins with the landside property line of the marina. This is the first line of defense in a layered or secured in-depth approach to the protection of a marina or any property or structure. The goal is to put in place many layers of security as part of an integrated security program for the maximum effect in deterring and detecting criminal activity and terrorism at the marina.

Based on the location of the marina, the threat assessment, and funding, the decision will be made to utilize only natural security barriers or to construct security barriers to secure the marina. For the most effective security of the marina and for safety and liability issues, it is always recommended that security barriers be constructed. This of course is a marina management decision that each maritime facility must make based on the threat, crime history, safety concerns, and availability of funding.

The goal of perimeter security barriers, natural or constructed, is to deter, delay, or detect access onto the marina property via the marina landside perimeter other than through the directed access control points such as roadways or pedestrian walkways. These access points can then be utilized for general observation of who is entering the marina property. The positive control is exemplified by the use of card access or the monitoring of the access points by a security officer or designated marina staff.

The use of natural security barriers, also known as Crime Prevention Through Environmental Design (CPTED), is most effective in the control of vehicle access to a property. Natural barriers such as streams, lakes, wetlands, rocks, trees, high-density undergrowth areas, and natural trenching in most situations will deter or prevent access onto a maritime landside property other than the designated access areas by vehicles. It could deter some individuals, but anyone wanting to walk onto the marina property will not be stopped by natural barriers. The fact that a marina is located on the water, that body of water serves as a natural barrier to most forms of access other than watercraft.

The most cost-effective constructed security barrier that can be used to protect the perimeter of a marina is chain link fencing. Chain link fencing is relatively low in cost compared to the construction of masonry walls. Chain link fencing provides the flexibility to move it as needed. Because one can see through the chain link fencing, it allows visibility beyond the marina property line by security, marina staff, and boat owners based at the marina. This visibility provides early warning to unauthorized access attempts onto the marina property and can result in the prevention of attempts to breach security at the marina.

With the visibility afforded beyond the marina property line by chain link fencing, other physical security measures can be integrated into the perimeter barrier. Use of security signage is easily accomplished by posting the signs on the security fence. Security lighting can not only light up the area at the fence but also beyond the marina property line for visibility at night.

Security cameras can be used on the perimeter of the marina and can see beyond the fence line, thus providing a deterrent and early warning of unauthorized access. Should access occur, the security cameras can record the incident for future identification and prosecution of the perpetrator of the incident at the marina.

Any security fencing installed on the perimeter marina property should meet the security industry standards for such fencing. Heavy gauge fencing needs to be used with an opening no larger than 2 inches.

The height of the fence should be at least 6 feet with a 1-foot top guard mounted at a 45° angle facing away from the property. The top guard is utilized to prevent an individual from climbing over the fence. The top guard needs to be constructed using barbed wire or razor ribbon.

The fence must be secured in the ground by metal posts with metal bracing bars or wire across the top and bottom of the fence. This is used to prevent the fencing from being pulled down or lifted up for access over the top or under the barrier (see Figure 6.4).

The perimeter fencing should be inspected daily for any signs of unauthorized entry, damage of the fence, or erosion under the fencing or around the fence post. To ensure visibility around the perimeter fencing and to prevent damage to the fence, a clear zone of 15–20 feet needs to be established on either side of the fence. The growth of trees close to the fence could be used as access portals over the top of the perimeter fencing.

Many marinas with fencing will provide a perimeter road, either stone or paving along the fence line. This allows for the easy inspection of the perimeter fence each day for security purposes. It also allows easy access for any grounds keeping in the clear zone or repair of the fence or other physical security devices integrated into the perimeter fence line.

FIGURE 6.4   Perimeter security fencing at Lakeside Marine, Harrisburg, Pennsylvania. (Photograph by Daniel J. Benny.)

Marina Access and Key Control

As stated previously, access control points such as roadways or pedestrian walkways allow for the general observation of who is entering the marina property. Vehicle and pedestrian access in most cases will be open to the public and tenants. This could include marina office personnel and other tenants such as a boating school, restaurant, or service provider operating at the marina.

Access control points can be utilized to facilitate positive control by the use of card access or monitoring of security cameras by a security officer or designated staff. This includes access to the boat docks, watercraft, boat storage areas, boat ramp areas, and fueling pumps.

When fencing is used at the marina pedestrian gates to control access to and from the boat ramp and dock areas, by boat owners and marina staff to access the secure area, the gate or gates can be controlled by the use of a proximity access cards and/or keys. It can also be controlled by remote access with the integration of the monitoring of security cameras by security or marina staff.

Access cards or keys to these areas need to be secured when not in use. They should only be issued to authorized individuals. This may include marina staff and boat owners.

Gates will also be required when fencing is used at marina to allow authorized vehicle access into the secure area of the marina. These vehicles many include those driven by boat owners, authorized vendors, marina or tenant staff, and emergency vehicles such as law enforcement, fire, or emergency medical services.

Access of vehicles at these access points with gates is best accomplished by the use of a proximity access card. Remote access can be used with the integration of the monitoring of security cameras by security or marina staff. This would limit the number of access cards or keys that are issued. The vehicle access points should also be covered by security cameras to monitor and record the activity. The security cameras should be monitored by marina security or staff.

If the marina perimeter is fenced, there needs to be at least two entrance points even if both are not used each day. It is important to have a secondary point of access should there be an emergency and access through the primary gate is denied.

Gates that are not used on a regular basis need to be secured with high-security padlocks. The locked gate should also be equipped with a numbered security seal. This security seal needs to be checked each day by security or marina staff to ensure the numbered seal is intact and matches the numbered seal placed on the gate. The use of a security seal and the daily inspection of the security seal will ensure that an unauthorized key is not being used so that a person can enter and exit the gate without detection. It is also used to ensure that the original padlock on the gate was not cut off and replaced with a different lock and then used by a perpetrator for continued unauthorized access into the marina or secure area.

Marina Security Signage

Signage is used at the marina to provide information. The information provided by signs may include services offered at the marina and driving and parking directions to control traffic. Signs can also be used to provide directions to locate marina facilities, tenant activity, docks, and water-craft operation areas. These signs, while not directly security related, do contribute to the security of the marina. This is because the signs begin the process of directing individuals and vehicles to areas of the marina where they are authorized. This would include the proper roadways to drive on, where to park a vehicle, and where an individual may walk about on the marina property in order to visit the office or other tenant activity. Other nonsecurity signage would include boater's information for operating on the ramps and around the docks and marina waterway.

Marinas should use signage to promote safety. This includes vehicle speed limit and traffic control signs. All vehicle traffic control signs on private property should meet the federal, local, and state department of transportation requirements. This is to ensure they are understood by the driver for the safety of all and for liability reasons. Other safety signs might include no smoking and directions to fire extinguishers. Safety-related signs may also be posted around the fueling pumps and boat operations area. Inside structure emergency exit signs will need to be installed.

The most important signs are those related to security. Security signage provides security information and warning to those entering the property. Security signage needs to begin on the marina perimeter. If there is a perimeter fencing, then the fence would be the best area to post security signs. If there is no fencing, then signs can be posted on sign poles around the perimeter of the property. These security signs should state *No Trespassing* to deter individuals from entering the boat operations areas such as the docks, boats, and ramps. The posting of such signs can prevent unauthorized access and if it does occur, can aid in the prosecution of the perpetrator for trespassing since it was legally posted. If the area is protected by security cameras, intrusion detection systems, or security patrols that information can also be posted on a security sign as a preventative measure. Never post anything about a security protection system that you do not have. Professional criminals will know that there is no protective equipment. It will only provide the marina with a false sense of security (see Figures 6.5 and 6.6).

FIGURE 6.5   Security sign outside the boathouse at Long Level Marina, Wrightsville, Pennsylvania. (Photograph by Daniel J. Benny.)

FIGURE 6.6   Security sign at Long Level Marina, Wrightsville, Pennsylvania. (Photograph by Daniel J. Benny.)

Additional examples of a sign could be as follows:

MARINA

PROPERTY

NO TRESPASSING

VIOLATORS WILL BE PROSECUTED

Security signage should include the U.S. Coast Guard America's Waterway Watch signs to show participation in the program.

Other locations for signs would be at the entrance to the marina, access to the boat operations, boat ramps, and fueling areas. These signs should state that authorized individuals and vehicles only are permitted into the area. Examples of signs for these areas are as follows:

MARINA BOAT OPERATIONS AREA
NO UNAUTHORIZED PERSONS
BEYOND THIS POINT

MARINA
RESTRICTED AREA
KEEP OUT

Signs should be very prominent and large at vehicle access points and around the perimeter of the marina. Smaller signs can be used in areas with only pedestrian access.

Marina Security Lighting

Security lighting takes away the sense of privacy of perpetrators that may consider entering the marina property at night. Security lighting also allows for better visibility with the use of security cameras, security patrols of the marina by security officers, marina staff, or drive-by law enforcement officers. Even boat owners going to and from their docks and boats can detect an unauthorized individual at the marina at night by seeing them on the marina property because of security lighting. Security lighting at the marina is a deterrent to crime. The lighting also provides a more safe and inviting environment to visitors, vendors, and boat owners.

Security lighting should be utilized on the perimeter of the marina to illuminate the boundary and fencing, if fencing is utilized. Security lighting needs to be used on all marina roadways, vehicle and pedestrian access points, and vehicle parking areas.

Buildings need to be illuminated with lighting. Entrance ways and doors should have effective lighting. The use of security lighting in the deterrence of crime against watercraft will also be part of the marina security lighting program. This would include boats in storage areas and at the docks.

Fuel storage areas where fuel pumps, storage tanks, or fueling trucks are located need to be well lit at night. This also includes chemical storage areas for working boats and boat repair services.

It is recommended that all security lighting be activated through the use of solar photocells so that the lights will activate automatically at night or during periods of low visibility due to fog or storms that may occur during daylight hours. This method of activation ensures that the security lighting is operating when it is needed.

All lighting units should be placed in protective housing to prevent damage. The lighting can be mounted on posts or the side of buildings. The lights should be spaced so that if one light is out, they are close enough to still illuminate the area until the light is operational. Each light should be numbered so that they can be easily identified and located on the marina security plan if they become inoperable. It is important to inspect the lights each night to ensure that they are all operating. Any inoperable light should be made operational as soon as possible.

Emergency lights need to be installed within the buildings that are occupied by individuals for easy egress during an emergency. A backup battery or fuel-powered generator power source is recommended to ensure that emergence lighting continues to work during a power outage. Critical security lighting can also be part of the emergency lighting backup system.

Marina Security Cameras

Security cameras aid in taking away the privacy of perpetrators that may consider entering the marina property. Security cameras allow for surveillance of the entire marina property or based on the threat and funding providing security coverage of specific high-risk areas such as watercraft storage, boat docks, or fuel storage. The security cameras provide a more safe and inviting environment to visitors, vendors, and watercraft owners (see Figures 6.7 and 6.8).

The use of security cameras can supplement the use of security patrols of the marina by security officers, marina staff, or drive-by law enforcement officers. Security cameras at the marina are a deterrent to crime. In addition to capturing events live, they can record the activity

FIGURE 6.7 Security camera at Long Level Marina, Wrightsville, Pennsylvania. (Photograph by Daniel J. Benny.)

FIGURE 6.8 Security cameras monitor the inside of the marina office at Long Level Marina, Wrightsville, Pennsylvania. (Photograph by Daniel J. Benny.)

observed for future use in the identification and apprehension of criminal suspect and for security modification to the security program.

Security cameras should be utilized on the perimeter of the marina to provide early warning of unauthorized access and to act as a deterrent to criminal or terrorist activity. Security cameras can also be utilized on roadways, vehicle and pedestrian access points, and vehicle parking areas.

Such buildings should have security camera coverage. Boathouses need to be included in the security camera coverage. Fuel storage areas where fuel pumps, storage tanks, or fueling trucks are located and chemical storage areas are important areas to place security cameras. This is not only for security reason but also for safety and fire protection issues.

All security cameras should be placed in a protective housing to prevent damage and provide protection from the weather. The security cameras can be mounted on posts or the sides of buildings. They should be spaced so that if one is out, they are close enough to still provide security of the area until the other camera is made operational. Each security camera should be numbered so that they can be easily identified and located on the marina security plan by the camera operator. This is also helpful to locate the cameras if they become inoperable. It is important to inspect the security cameras each day to ensure that they are all operating. Any inoperable security camera should be made operational as soon as possible.

Security of the Docks

All access points from the marina property to the watercraft at the dock or boat ramp should be secured and monitored. These entry points should only be accessible to marina staff and boat owners.

Only authorized vehicles that have been properly identified and approved by the marina should be permitted near the boat ramp area and docks. This would include passenger transport vehicles driven by boat owners and cleared limousines, rental cars, and service vehicles. Taxicabs and other vendors should never be permitted to enter the boat ramp under any circumstances. The marina should require authorized marina vehicles accessing the boat ramp area or docks to be driven by properly trained and credentialed individuals. They should be wearing a valid marina security badge that authorizes their presence within that area of the marina.

Security of Boat Storage Areas

Boat and land storage areas are for the placement of transit watercraft or long-term and seasonal land storage. Access needs to be controlled into this area and needs to be secured and limited to only authorized individuals. This would include the boat owners and marina staff.

Only authorized vehicles that have been properly identified and approved by the marina manager should be permitted into the area. This would include passenger transport vehicles driven by pilots and boat owners and cleared limousines, rental cars, and service vehicles.

Security of Fueling Facilities

Fueling facilities at marinas need to be considered as part of the security program. Most often, fuel may be disbursed by the use of self-service fuel pumps with in-ground fuel tanks. This method is where the boat owner will fuel the boat themselves with no assistance. Utilizing the self-service method reduces the security of the fueling area (see Figure 6.9).

If the fuel pumps are used for self-service, fuel security controls must be in place at the pumps. Keys can be signed out for the boater to fuel the watercraft and then return the keys. Card readers could be utilized for boaters to obtain fuel through the self-service method. It is recommended that the marina operate the fuel pumps and if that is not possible.

When the marina is closed, the nozzles of the fuel pumps should be locked in place with a padlock. The fuel pumps should also have an electric cutoff switch to turn off power to the fuel pumps. This will prevent theft of fuel and safety and fire hazards at the fuel pumps.

FIGURE 6.9 Boat fueling dock at Long Level Marina, Wrightsville, Pennsylvania. (Photograph by Daniel J. Benny.)

Security of Chemical Storage Tanks

Chemicals associated with boat cleaning and repair operations should be stored in locked facilities. They can also be stored in a fenced area that includes access-controlled gates, security signage, lighting, and the use of security cameras. Only authorized individuals should be permitted to enter the secure area where the chemical storage tanks are located. All access ports to the chemical storage tanks need to be locked.

Marina Internet Security

With the widespread use of the Internet in the maritime community, an entire new area for criminal activity and misuse has been created. In order to know how to protect the marina's assets, it is vital that there is an understanding of the threat.

Protection of the Internet and the information which can be retrieved, manipulated, or removed is complex. There are loose rules and regulations for these systems worldwide; therefore, security is the end-system user's responsibility. The threat to the system at the marina is the information that can be stolen by hackers, competitors, customers or clients, contractors, or employees. They can wreak havoc on the Internet through the destruction or modification of data, copying, stealing, denial of service, compromising valuable resources, counterfeiting of checks or credit cards, destructive manipulation by the use of Trojan horses, logic bombs or viruses, and the transmission of contraband. Such activity is considered computer crime, which is any crime where a computer is used as a primary or secondary in the commission of a crime.

While most states have laws relating to computer crime, it is also a federal offense and falls under Title 18, Section 1030 and Title 18, Section 2701. The Federal Bureau of Investigation (FBI) has primary jurisdiction over all traditional investigations related to national defense, foreign relations, or any restricted data which can be used to cause damage to the United States. The U.S. Secret Service has primary jurisdiction over criminal acts involving consumer reporting or U.S. Treasury computers. The FBI and the U.S. Secret Service have concurrent jurisdiction over financial institutions fraud.

While developing a security program, one must conduct a risk assessment based on the projected use of the Internet and possible risk. Develop the marina Internet security policy based on the greatest risk and implement controls to enforce the policy. As part of the security controls, have at least two levels of protection for the most sensitive information and treat the infrastructure and applications as two distinct but mutually dependent areas. In keeping with the security consultant who coined the phrase "loss prevention" in the 1960s, Sal Astor's Fifth Law of Loss Prevention, "any loss prevention control fails only upon audit." Ensure that there are strict monitoring and reporting procedures to support their security policy. Issues to consider are what services are allowed, what services or sites will be blocked, what is considered acceptable usage of employee e-mail, and how will the policy be enforced.

As part of the protection plan, minimize the number of connections to the Internet at the marina and control them. Increase the security of each connected computer and strengthen the network perimeter. The key is to keep outsiders out, but allow insiders to roam freely without doing any damage.

To allow insiders to roam freely and still provide protection of information, one must restrict access to key sensitive assets and minimize the impact of a penetration as most penetrations are from insiders or hackers masquerading as insiders. It is important to provide access control on servers and only allow authorized users access to sensitive information.

Segregate functions and areas by the use of firewalls, which are hardware/software systems that regulate communications between networks. The firewall philosophy should be that which is not expressly permitted is prohibited. Firewalls can filter network traffic based on the security policy and can detect potential hackers before they break in. While firewalls can provide protection, remember that 80% of all penetrations are from insiders and 30% occur after a firewall has been installed. A firewall will not automatically detect an attempted break-in and may not be correctly configured. Intruders can go into a network directly, bypassing the firewall altogether with an end run.

The key factors in the protection of marina assets through the Internet are the development of a sound security policy and the use of proxy firewalls when possible. Ensure that the firewall software is up to date and examine the security of modem connections to avoid end runs. Conduct inspections and penetration testing software against your system. Use of programs such as McAfee that are available for sale or free programs such as Spybot can detect and eliminate threats to your marina computer. By following these guidelines, one can reduce the threat of loss through the Internet at the marina.

BIBLIOGRAPHY

International Maritime Organization. (2012). *Guide to maritime security and the ISPS code.* London, UK: Author.

United States Coast Guard. (2002). *Maritime strategy for homeland security.* Washington, DC: U.S. Government Printing Office.

United States Coast Guard. (2014). *United States counter piracy and maritime security action plan*. Washington, DC: U.S. Government Printing Office.
United States Department of Homeland Security. (2008). *Small vessel security strategy*. Washington, DC: U.S. Government Printing Office.

CHAPTER 7

Port Facility Security

PORT FACILITY SECURITY OFFICER
AND SECURITY FORCE

According to the International Maritime Organization (IMO) International Ship and Port Facility Security Code (ISPS Code), the port facility needs to identify an individual as the Port Facility Security Officer. This person will be responsible for the development, implementation, revision, and maintenance of the security department and port facility security plan. The Port Facility Security Officer will also be the liaison with the ship and ship company security officers. A security professional should be selected for the position of Facility Security Officer.

The size and type of security department at the port facility will be the decision of Port Facility Security Officer and senior management of the port based on a risk assessment, size of the port, type of operations and shippers at the port facility, the location of the port, and budget.

Security awareness is the first line of defense in the protection of the port facility. To be effective, the entire maritime community at the port facility must be involved. Adoption of the U.S. Coast Guard America's Waterway Watch program is recommended. To enhance this security awareness, the U.S. Coast Guard America's Waterway Watch program encompasses two concepts related to security, physical security, and security awareness. As it relates to physical security, the program recommends and encourages the maritime community to utilize physical security practices to prevent and reduce crime by securing boats and marinas.

The security awareness aspect of the program focuses on making marina owners and employees, as well as boat owners and seaplane pilots, aware of their surroundings. This includes being aware of what is considered normal activity at the marina and surrounding maritime

FIGURE 7.1   The U.S. Coast Guard America's Waterway Watch program
sign. (Photograph by Daniel J. Benny.)

environment and what is not. Promote security by the use of U.S. Coast
Guard America's Waterway Watch program sign (see Figure 7.1).

TRAINING OF THE SECURITY FORCE

As specified in the ISPS Code, port security personnel are required
to be trained. This includes full-time, part-time, or contractor port
facility security personnel. This required training includes the provisions of the port security plan and understanding of the Maritime
Security (MARSEC) Levels, the Transportation Worker's Identification
Credential program, as well as recognition of dangerous substances and
devices that would be a threat to the port or vessels docked at the port.

All of the port facility security staff must receive initial and then
annual security training. Port facility security personnel must also receive
specialized training related to specific security assignments at the time
they are assigned to such functions. Documentation of all security training must be recorded and documented by the port security officer.

PORT FACILITY SECURITY ASSESSMENT

It is vital to develop an adequate port facility security plan. To develop such a plan, a port security assessment must be conducted. The goal is to have a security and safety environment that allows for the normal operations of the port and its mission. The port facility security assessment allows the security department to be proactive against criminal activity, piracy, and terrorism rather than reactive. Being proactive reduces risk and should an incident occur it fosters a more positive outcome.

The port facility security assessment is accomplished by conducting a comprehensive review of the security threats and vulnerabilities of the port facility based on the type of port, the vessels that visit the port, its mission, cargo, and area of operations. Based on the results of this security risk assessment, the size of the security and type physical security measures can be determined, which provide the adequate countermeasures based on the risk and threats to the port facility, staff, crews, and vessel in port.

The port facility security assessment is an ongoing process and not just a onetime event. At a minimum, a port facility security assessment needs to be conducted at least once a year. When a security incident occurs, a review of the incident should be conducted. The purpose is to see how security department and the security plan performed during the incident. This is an excellent opportunity for an updated security assessment.

The U.S. Coast Guard MARSEC Levels should be considered when conducting the assessment and plan.

MARSEC Level 1 means the level for which minimum appropriate protective security measures shall be maintained at all times. This is the level at which ships and port facilities normally operate.

MARSEC Level 2 means the level for which appropriate additional protective security measures shall be maintained for a period of time as a result of heightened risk of a security incident. This is a heightened level of awareness and precautionary activity applying for as long as there is a heightened security risk.

MARSEC Level 3 means the level for which further specific protective security measures shall be maintained for a limited period of time when a security incident is probable or imminent, although it may not be possible to identify the specific target. This is an exceptionally high level of awareness and precautionary activity for a period of time when there is an imminent risk of a security incident.

PORT FACILITY SECURITY PLAN

According to the IMO ISPS Code, the Port Facility Security Plan must be developed to ensure the application of measures designed to protect the port facility and ships, persons, cargo, cargo transport units, and ships stored within a port facility from the risks of a security incident. The Marine Transportation Security Regulations, when promulgated, will refer to a Facility Security Plan, in keeping with the Marine Transportation Security Act, which refers to Marine Facilities.

The Port Facility Security Officer is the person designated as responsible for the development, implementation, revision, and maintenance of the Port Facility Security Plan and for liaison with hip's security officers and company security officers.

The Port Facility Security Plan will provide the blueprint to protect the facility assets, employees, visitors, customer, and vessels located at the port facility against crime, sabotage, piracy, and terrorism. It is important that the Port Facility Security Plan include not only security measures to prevent security events, but also how to respond if such an event occurs. This will include working closely with the U.S. Coast Guard and other federal, state, and local law enforcement agencies. This interagency communication must also include the port authority, local fire, and emergency response agencies. The goal of the Port Facility Security Plan is to mitigate the risks identified in the Port Facility Security Assessment. The port facility owner or operator has the primary authority for ensuring the security of the port facility.

As stated in the IMO ISPS Code, the Port Facility Security Plan should at a minimum include the following important information:

- *Physical Security*: Physical security and measures and equipment provided to deter or delay the unauthorized carriage of weapons, dangerous substances, and devices intended for use against people, vessels, or ports.
- *Restricted Areas*: The designation of the restricted areas of the port facility and the measures and physical security devices for the prevention of unauthorized access to the port facility and to restricted areas of the port facility.
- *Evacuation of the Port Facility*: Procedures for evacuation of the port facility in the event of security threats or breaches of security at the port facility are the responsibilities of port facility security department members.
- *Auditing Procedures*: Procedures for auditing the security activities, procedures for training, exercises, and drills associated with the plan, interfacing with port vessel security

members and activity must also be included in the Port Facility Security Plan.

- *Security Incidents*: Additional procedures covering reporting transportation security incidents and summoning emergency, safety, or security personnel including local fire and police departments, bomb disposal units, divers, hospital, and emergency medical services. Other procedures should include the identification of the Facility Security Officer and the availability of a 24-hour a day contact for emergencies. Measures need to be established to ensure the security of the information contained in the plan and procedures for auditing the facility plan. Procedures for responding in case a ship's security alert system is activated.

PHYSICAL SECURITY OF THE PORT AND PORT FACILITY

The physical security measures addressed in Chapter 4 of this book can be used for the development of a physical security program at the port' facility. This includes locks, access controls, intrusion detection systems, security cameras, security lighting, and shore-based and water-based physical barriers.

Perimeter Security

The perimeter security of the port facility begins with the landside property line of the port facility. This is the first line of defense in a layered or secured in-depth approach to the protection of the port and its structures. The goal is to put in place many layers of security a part of an integrated security program for the maximum effect in deterring and detecting criminal activity and terrorism at the port facility.

Based on the location of the port, the threat assessment, and funding, the decision will be made to utilize only natural security barriers or to construct security barriers to secure the port. For the most effective security of the port facility and for safety and liability issues, security barriers should be constructed.

The goal of perimeter security barriers, natural or constructed, is to deter, delay, or detect access onto the port facility. These access points can then be utilized for general observation of who is entering the marina property. The positive control is exemplified by the use of card access or the monitoring of the access points by a security officer or designated port facility staff.

The use of natural security barriers, also known as Crime Prevention Through Environmental Design (CPTED), is most effective in the control of vehicle access to the property. Natural barriers such as streams, lakes, wetlands, rocks, trees, high-density undergrowth areas, and natural trenching in most situations will deter or prevent access onto the port landside property other than the designated access areas by vehicles. It could deter some individuals, but anyone wanting to walk onto the marina property will not be stopped by natural barriers. The fact that a marina is located on the water, that body of water serves as a natural barrier to most forms of access other than watercraft.

The most cost-effective constructed security barrier that can be used to protect the perimeter of a port facility is chain link fencing. Chain link fencing is relatively low in cost compared to the construction of masonry walls and provides the flexibility to be moved as needed. Because one can see through a chain link fencing, it allows visibility beyond the marina property line by security, marina staff, and boat owners based at the marina. This visibility provides early warning to unauthorized access attempts onto the marina property and can result in the prevention of such attempts to breach security at the marina (see Figure 7.2).

With the visibility afforded beyond the port facility property line by chain link fencing, other physical security measures can be integrated

FIGURE 7.2 Security fencing at a port facility, Philadelphia, Pennsylvania. (Photograph by Daniel J. Benny.)

with the perimeter barrier. Use of security signage is easily accomplished by posting the signs on the security fence. Security lighting can not only light up the area at the fence but also beyond the marina property line for visibility at night.

Security cameras can be used on the perimeter of the marina and can see beyond the fence line, thus providing a deterrent and early warning of unauthorized access. If access occurs, the security cameras can record the incident for future identification and prosecution of the perpetrator of the incident at the port.

Any security fencing installed on the perimeter port facility should meet the security industry standards for such fencing. Heavy gauge fencing needs to be used with an opening no larger than 2 inches. The height of the fence should be at least 6 feet with a 1-foot top guard mounted at a 45° angle facing away from the property. The top guard is utilized to prevent an individual from climbing over the fence. The top guard needs to be constructed of barbed wire or razor ribbon.

The fence must be secured in the ground by metal posts with metal bracing bars or wire across the top and bottom of the fence. This is used to prevent the fencing from being pulled down or lifted up for access over the top or under the barrier.

The perimeter fencing should be inspected daily for any signs of unauthorized entry, damage of the fence or erosion under the fencing or around the fence post. To ensure visibility around the perimeter fencing and to prevent damage to the fence, a clear zone of 15–20 feet needs to be established on either side of the fence. The growth of trees close to the fence could be used as access portals over the top of the perimeter fencing.

Many port facilities with fencing will provide a perimeter road, either stone or paving along the fence line. This allows for the easy inspection of the perimeter fence each day for security purposes. It also allows easy access for any grounds keeping in the clear zone or repair of the fence or other physical security devices integrated into the perimeter fence line.

Port Facility Access and Key Control

As stated previously, access control points such as roadways or pedestrian walkways allow for the general observation of who is entering the port facility. Vehicle and pedestrian access in most cases will be open to public parking areas and entrances into buildings for tenants. This could include port facility management, office personnel, and other tenants.

Access control points can be utilized to facilitate positive control by the use of card access or monitoring of security cameras by a security officer or designated port security staff in areas that require higher security. This includes access to the docks, ships at the port, high-risk storage, and fueling areas.

When fencing is used at the port facility, pedestrian gates to control access to and from the facility or restricted areas can be controlled by the use of a proximity access cards and keys. It can also be controlled by remote access with the integration of the monitoring of security cameras by security or port facility staff. Access cards or keys to these areas need to be secured when not in use. They should only be issued to authorized individuals.

Gates will also be required when fencing is used at a port facility to allow authorized vehicle access into the secure areas of the port.

Access of vehicles at these access points with gates is best accomplished by the use of a proximity access cards. Remote access can be used with the integration of the monitoring of security cameras by security or port facility staff. This would limit the number of access cards or keys that are issued. The vehicle access points should also be covered by security cameras to monitor and record the activity. The security cameras should be monitored by port security or staff.

When a port facility has a fenced perimeter, there needs to be at least two entrance points even if both are not used each day. It is important to have a secondary point of access should there be an emergency and access through the primary gate is denied.

Gates that are not used on a regular basis need to be secured with a high-security padlock. The locked gate should also be equipped with a numbered security seal. This security seal needs to be checked each day by security or port facility staff to ensure the numbered seal is intact and matches the numbered seal placed on the gate. The use of a security seal and the daily inspection of the security seal will ensure that an unauthorized key is not being used so that a person can enter and exit the gate without detection. It is also used to ensure that the original padlock on the gate was not cut off and replaced with a different lock and then used by a perpetrator for continued unauthorized access into the port facility.

Port Facility Security Signage

Signage is used at the port to provide information. The information provided by signs may include services offered at the marina and driving and parking directions to control traffic. Signs can also be used to provide directions to locate port facilities, tenant activity, docks, and ship operation areas. These signs, while not directly security related, do contribute to the security of the port. This is because the signs begin the process of directing individuals and vehicles to areas of the port where they are authorized. This would include the proper roadways to drive on, where to park a vehicle, and where an individual may walk about on the marina property in order to visit the office or other tenant activity. Other nonsecurity signage would include boater's information for operating on the ramps and around the docks and port waterway.

The port facility should use signage to promote safety. This would include vehicle speed limit and traffic control signs. All vehicle traffic control signs on private property should meet federal, state, and local department of transportation requirements. This is to ensure that they are understood by the driver for the safety of all and for liability reasons. Other safety signs might include no smoking and directions to fire extinguishers. Safety-related signs may also be posted around the fueling pumps and ship operation areas. Inside structure emergency exit signs will need to be installed.

The most important signs are those related to security. Security signage provides security information and warning to those entering the marina property. Security signage needs to begin on the port perimeter. If there is perimeter fencing, then the fence would be the best area to post security signs. If there is no fencing, then signs can be posted on sign poles around the perimeter of the property. These security signs should state *No Trespassing* to deter individuals from entering the boat operation areas such as the docks, boats, and ramps. The posting of such signs can prevent unauthorized access and if it does occur, it can aid in the prosecution of the perpetrator for trespassing since it was legally posted. If the area is protected by security cameras, intrusion detection systems, and security patrols, those information can also be posted on a security sign as a preventative measure.

Additional examples of a sign would be as follows:

PORT PROPERTY

NO TRESPASSING

VIOLATORS WILL BE PROSECUTED

PORT

RESTRICTED AREA

KEEP OUT

Signs should be very prominent and large at vehicle access points and around the perimeter of the marina. Smaller signs can be used in areas with only pedestrian access.

Port Facility Security Lighting

Security lighting takes away the sense of privacy of perpetrators that may consider entering the port facility at night. Security lighting also allows for better visibility with the use of security cameras, security patrols of the marina by security officers, or drive-by law enforcement officers. The lighting also provides a more safe and inviting environment.

Security lighting should be utilized on the perimeter of the port facility to illuminate the boundary and fencing, if fencing is utilized. Security lighting needs to be used on all roadways, vehicle and pedestrian access points, and vehicle parking areas.

Buildings need to be illuminated with lighting. Entrance ways and doors should have effective lighting. The use of security lighting in the deterrence of crime against ships at the port will also be part of the security lighting program and would include dock lighting.

Fuel storage areas where fuel pumps, storage tanks, or fueling trucks are located need to be well lit at night. This would also include chemical storage areas for working ships and ship repair services.

FIGURE 7.3   Security lighting at a port facility, San Diego, California. (Photograph by Daniel J. Benny.)

It is recommended that all security lighting be activated through the use of solar photocells so that the lights will activate automatically at night or during periods of low visibility due to fog or storms that may occur during daylight hours. This method of activation ensures that the security lighting is operating when it is needed (see Figure 7.3).

All lighting units should be placed in protective housings to prevent damage. The lighting can be mounted on posts or the side of building. The lights should be spaced so that if one light is out, they are close enough to still illuminate the area until the light is operational. Each light should be numbered so that they can be easily identified and located on the port facility security plan if they become inoperable. It is important to inspect the lights each night to ensure that they are all operating. Any inoperable light should be made operational as soon as possible.

Emergency lights need to be installed within the buildings that are occupied by individuals for easy egress during an emergency. A backup battery or fuel-powered generator power source is recommended to ensure that emergency lighting continues to work during a power outage. Critical security lighting can also be a part of the emergency lighting backup system.

Port Facility Security Cameras

Security cameras aid in taking away the privacy of perpetrators that may consider entering the port facility property. Security cameras allow for surveillance of the entire property. The security cameras provide a more safe and inviting environment to visitors, vendors, and watercraft owners (see Figure 7.4).

The use of security cameras can supplement the use of security patrols of the port by security officers or drive-by law enforcement officers. Security cameras at the port are a deterrent to crime. In addition to capturing events live, they can record the activity observed for future use in the identification and apprehension of criminal suspect and for security modification to the security program.

Security cameras should be utilized on the perimeter of the port facility to provide early warning of unauthorized access and to act as a deterrent to criminal or terrorist activity. They can also be utilized on roadways, vehicle and pedestrian access points, and vehicle parking areas.

Such buildings should have security camera coverage. Fuel storage areas where fuel pumps, storage tanks, or fueling trucks are located and chemical storage areas are important areas to place security cameras. All dock areas should have security camera coverage.

FIGURE 7.4   Security camera mounted on a structure at a port facility, Pensacola, Florida. (Photograph by Daniel J. Benny.)

All security cameras should be placed in protective housing to prevent damage and provide protection from the weather. The security cameras can be mounted on posts or the side of building. They should be spaced so that if one is out, they are close enough to still provide security of the area until the other camera is made operational. Each security camera should be numbered so that they can be easily identified and located on the port facility security plan by the camera operator. This is also helpful to locate the cameras if they become inoperable. It is important to inspect the security cameras each day to ensure that they are all operating. Any inoperable security cameras should be made operational as soon as possible.

SECURITY OF THE DOCKS

All access points from the port facility property to the ships at the dock should be secured and monitored. These entry points should only be accessible to authorized individuals. The port facility should require authorized port vehicles accessing the docks to be driven by properly trained and credentialed individuals. They should be wearing a valid port security badge that authorizes their presence within that area of the docks with the vehicle.

SECURITY OF PORT FACILITY
CHEMICAL STORAGE TANKS

Chemicals associated with boat cleaning and repair operations should be stored in locked facilities. They can also be stored in a fenced area that includes access controlled gates, security signage, lighting, and the use of security cameras. Only authorized individuals should be permitted to enter the secure area where the chemical storage tanks are located. All access ports to the chemical storage tanks need to be locked.

PORT FACILITY INTERNET SECURITY

With the widespread use of the Internet in the maritime community, an entire new area for criminal activity and misuse has been created. In order to know how to protect the port facility, it is vital to have an understanding of the threat.

Protection of the Internet and the information that can be retrieved, manipulated, or removed is complex. There are loose rules and regulations for the systems worldwide; therefore, security is the end-system user's responsibility. The threat to the system at the port facility is the information that can be stolen by hackers, competitors, customers or clients, contractors or employees. They can wreak havoc on the net through the destruction or modification of data, copying or stealing it, denial of service or compromising valuable resources, counterfeiting of checks or credit cards, destructive manipulation by the use of Trojan horses, logic bombs or viruses, and the transmission of contraband. Such activity is considered computer crime, which is any crime where a computer is used as a primary or secondary in the commission of a crime.

As mentioned in a previous chapter, most states have laws relating to computer crime. It is also a federal offense and falls under Title 18, Section 1030 and Title 18, Section 2701. The Federal Bureau of Investigation (FBI) has primary jurisdiction over all traditional investigations related to national defense, foreign relations, or any restricted data that can be used to cause damage to the United States. The U.S. Secret Service has primary jurisdiction over criminal acts involving consumer reporting or U.S. Treasury computers. The FBI and the U.S. Secret Service have concurrent jurisdiction over financial institutions fraud.

While developing a security program, one must conduct a risk assessment based on the projected use of the Internet and possible risk. Develop the port facility Internet security policy based on the greatest risk and implement controls to enforce the policy. As part of the security controls, have at least two levels of protection for the most sensitive information. As always and in keeping with of the security consultant who coined the phrase "loss prevention" in the 1960s, the Sal Astor's Fifth Law of Loss Prevention, "any loss prevention control fails only upon audit." Ensure that there are strict monitoring and reporting procedures to support the security policy.

As part of the protection plan, minimize the number of connections to the Internet at the port facility. Increase the security of each connected computer and strengthen the network perimeter. The key is to keep outsiders out, but allow insiders to roam freely without doing any damage.

Segregate functions and areas by the use of firewalls, which are hardware/software systems that regulate communications between networks. The firewall philosophy should be that which is not expressly permitted is prohibited. Firewalls can filter network traffic based on the security policy and can detect potential hackers before they break in. While firewalls can provide protection, remember that 80% of all penetrations are from insiders and 30% occur after a firewall has been installed. A firewall will not automatically detect an attempted break-in, and may not be correctly configured. Intruders can go into a network directly, bypassing the firewall altogether with an end run.

PORT FACILITY SECURITY COMMUNICATIONS

It is important that the port facility have an effective two-way communications system to not only deal with the operation of the port but also during the time of emergencies, especially piracy or terrorism incidents.

A security radio communications system is the primary means of security communication at the port facility. The port's phone or intercom can be used as a backup means of communication. Radio contact must be maintained during all operations and this is even more important during security incidents. Communications between port facility and incoming ships will be by VHF radio communications and must be maintained at all times during a security situation.

PORT FACILITY SECURITY ADMINISTRATION

It is a requirement of the Port Security Officer to keep records of all security-related information and activity. These records may be kept in hard copy or in electronic format. All security information must be protected from unauthorized access. All electronic-formatted information must be protected from unauthorized access, deletion, destruction, or amendment.

The information that must be kept includes all reports of security incidents, including criminal activity, piracy, or terrorism. Any security threats to the port or ships in port must be documented as well as change in the MARSEC Level of the port facility or a specific ship in port based on the incident or threat. A ship Declaration of Security and the reason for the Declaration must also be maintained by the Port Security Officer.

All information and records related to security training should include the date, location, duration, and subject matter of the training as well as who attended and passed the program. All security exercises and drills must also be documented, which include the date, scenario, and the outcome of the exercises or drills. Any lessons learned or best practices must also be documented. The ports' annual or any periodic security audits and threat assessments must also be documented.

PORT FACILITY EMERGENCY SECURITY DRILLS AND EXERCISES

Emergency security drills and exercises are important in any security environment, which include the port or port facility. The port facility security force must take immediate action to thwart a threat. One of the best methods of ensuring a rapid and effective response by the port's security force is to have frequent security exercises and drills so that all members of the force will know their role in such an event. It also allows for the honing of the security plan so that changes can be made to enhance performance during a real security incident.

It is a requirement that security drills and exercises be conducted at least once every 3 months. The drill must test all the components of the port's security plan and security force.

Security drills and exercises need to be varied in time, location in the port, and type of security situation. It may be a tabletop simulation, a seminar, or a full-scale live drill and exercise. Once each drill or exercise has been completed, it must be evaluated to determine the success of the event. Any positive or negative aspects of the drill or exercise need to be documented. Improvement should be made based on the result of drills or exercises.

U.S. NAVY PHYSICAL SECURITY AT PRIVATE CONTRACTOR'S FACILITIES

Port facilities that have contracts with the U.S. Navy for ship repair or other maritime-related services must follow the requirements of the U.S. Navy Physical Security at Private Contractor's Facilities.

The basic requirements are that the port facility must meet the requirements of the force protection measures under Force Protection Conditions such as Normal, Alpha, Bravo, Charlie, and Delta, respectively. The port facility must provide a written plan that shall be implemented for the protection of personnel, U.S. Naval vessels, and the material and equipment to be installed at the contractor's facility (see Appendix E).

BIBLIOGRAPHY

International Maritime Organization. (2012). *Guide to maritime security and the ISPS code.* London, UK: Author.
Mid-Atlantic Maritime Academy. (2012). *Vessel security officer.* Virginia Beach, VA: Author.
United States Department of Homeland Security. (2008). *Small vessel security strategy.* Washington, DC: U.S. Government Printing Office.

CHAPTER 8

Small Watercraft and Yacht Security

SHIPBOARD PHYSICAL SECURITY

Physical security of small watercraft consists of a variety of security methods. The goal is to provide in-depth security in order to prevent or reduce losses. For all watercraft it is important to remove the keys when not in use and for boats with compartments to ensure that they are locked with high-security locks.

Boats with an outboard engine should have the engine secured to the stern of the boat with a security chain and high-security padlock to prevent easy removal and theft of the engine. It is important to keep a record of the outboard engine serial number to aid in identification if stolen. To prevent a boat from being started and then stolen as mentioned earlier it should be kept locked and keys removed. Additional measures could include a hidden fuel cutoff switch to prevent the engine from being started. The use of an intrusion detection system and security cameras on cabin boats will also aid in the prevention of the theft of the boat or valuables stored in the cabin. Security seals can also be placed on cabin doors and hatches to deter theft or to at least know if an unauthorized individual entered the cabin of the boat or yacht.

All portholes or methods of viewing into a locked watercraft cabin should be constructed of tinted glass or covered from the inside to prevent viewing into the vessels where valuables and electronics can be seen. If valuables or electronics can be viewed from outside the boat, it makes the watercraft a more tempting target for theft.

Maintain an inventory of all marine electronics installed on the boat. Mark all marine electronics with an identifiable mark. Record serial numbers of the equipment. Should the equipment be stolen and recovered by police the marking of the equipment and the record of the serial numbers will aid in the recovery of the equipment to the owner.

Keep a record of the Hull Identification Number (HIN). This is a number stamped onto the hull of the watercraft, which can be used for positive identification if the boat is stolen or lost in bad weather.

SECURITY AND CREW SELECTION

On larger private boats and yachts, a crew or even a captain may be hired to operate the vessel for the owners of the watercraft. In addition to the maritime certifications and licenses that may be required, it is important to conduct a criminal and reference background investigation of the crew. This can be done by the owner or by contracting the services of a professional licensed private investigator.

There are individuals who will seek employment on private yachts for the purpose of theft of property or the watercraft. Other criminal activity may be to facilitate piracy or even terrorism by being selected as a member of the crew of the yacht. This would give them the opportunity to circumvent the security of the vessel.

SECURITY AT MARINAS

Marina selection is the key to the security of one's watercraft. Based on the area, there may be a limited selection of marinas to dock or store a boat, in fact there may only be one in a given area. This is especially true

FIGURE 8.1   Pennsylvania Fish and Boat Commission patrol boat used to patrol nearby marinas in Middletown, Pennsylvania. (Photograph by Daniel J. Benny.)

with inland boating on lakes and rivers. If there is a choice, a marina with adequate security should be selected.

Select a marina that takes part in the U.S. Coast Guard America's Waterway Watch program. This demonstrates that the marina is proactive and is aware of the various security threats. Look for a marina with some perimeter security protection to include fencing, lighting, access control, signs, and security cameras. Docks should be protected with security cameras, signs, and security lighting. It is important that the marina is patrolled by security or at least marina staff. Any local law enforcement patrols of the marina areas will provide additional security and aid in loss prevention (see Figure 8.1).

SMALL WATERCRAFT TRAILER AND STORAGE SECURITY

Small watercraft are often stored on a boat trailer all, or part, of the year. If a perpetrator wants to steal a boat, they can just hitch the boat trailer to their vehicle and drive off with it. Security methods to prevent such a theft include the use of a boat trailer hitch lock. The lock slides over the end of the hitch and prevents the trailer from being attached to a vehicle (see Figures 8.2 and 8.3). A trailer wheel boot can also be used. This security device is attached to the wheel of the trailer to prevent it from being towed away by preventing the wheel from turning.

FIGURE 8.2   Boat trailer with a hitch lock. (Photograph by Daniel J. Benny.)

FIGURE 8.3   Boat trailer with a hitch lock. (Photograph by Daniel J. Benny.)

FIGURE 8.4   Boat security with shrink-wrap for long-term or winter storage. (Photograph by Daniel J. Benny.)

In addition to the use of a hitch lock and/or wheel boot, if possible, the trailer and boat should be secured in a garage or inside a boathouse with locking doors that has an intrusion detection system and security cameras. If this is not possible, then the trailer and boat could be placed inside of an area protected by chain link fencing with a locked gate with security lighting and security cameras.

If stored outdoors during the off-boating season, the boat and trailer could be covered with shrink-wrap. This will protect the boat not only from the weather but also from vandalism and possible theft from onboard the watercraft (see Figure 8.4).

BIBLIOGRAPHY

United States Department of Homeland Security. (2008). *Small vessel security strategy*. Washington, DC: U.S. Government Printing Office.

United States Power Squadron/University of West Florida. (2012). USPS University/University of West Florida Seminar Small Boat Security. Pensacola, FL: University of West Florida.

CHAPTER 9

Ship Security

VESSEL AND COMPANY SECURITY OFFICER AND VESSEL SECURITY PERSONNEL

Vessel Security Officer

As specified in the ISPS Code, each ship or vessel as described in the Code is to designate an individual as the vessel security officer. The responsibilities include administration of the security force and the development and implementation of the ship security plan. The vessel security officer is also responsible for ensuring that a security assessment for the ship is conducted and that an ongoing security inspection program is carried out. The vessel security officer conducts investigations into security violations and incidents that occur onboard the vessel. The utilization of adequate physical security measures for the ship and the training of the security force is part of the vessel security function. Often the vessel security officer is a collateral assignment. It is recommended that a security professional be hired for this position to ensure the security of the ship. The vessel security officer must be able to obtain a Transportation Worker Identification Credential (TWIC).

Company Security Officer

Each shipping company is required to designate an individual as the company security officer as specified in the ISPS Code. The company security officer may be responsible for one or more ships depending on the size of the company. The functions of the company security officer are to coordinate security and support the vessel security officers and to establish company security guidelines in accordance with the ISPS Code. In addition, he or she should provide advice with regard to security threat levels and ensure that the ship security assessments and inspections are being carried out.

The establishment of a company security training program for all security including vessel security should be developed and provided to vessel security officers and security staff. Often, the company security officer is a collateral assignment. It is recommended that a security profession be hired for this position to ensure the security of the ships and company facility. The company security officer must be able to obtain a Transportation Worker Identification Credential.

Vessel and Company Security Personnel

The role of vessel and company security personnel is to provide protection of the vessel through proactive patrols and response to security incidents. As specified in the ISPS Code, vessel and company security personnel must be able to obtain a Transportation Worker Identification Credential and must have a thorough knowledge of security functions and current security threats and patterns.

They need to understand and have knowledge of current physical security measures, characteristics, and behavioral patterns of possible criminal or terrorist suspects. The vessel and company security personnel must be able to effectively deal with crowd management, emergency procedures, and all aspects of the vessel security plan.

Vessel and company security personnel do not in most cases carry firearms. This is because they are most often prohibited from being carried in the countries of various ports of departure and entry where the security personnel would be deployed. Violations of such firearms laws can have severe penalties, including a long prison sentence. In some counties, it is considered a capital offense. Commercial shipping companies will not risk violating the firearms laws of other countries. However, the risk is that there is less protection in hostile waters from the threat of pirates or terrorists, who are aware that mariners on such vessels are normally unarmed. The carrying of firearms by vessel security personnel is the decision of the vessel company and the ship's captain.

TRAINING OF THE SECURITY FORCE

As specified in the ISPS Code, vessel and company security personnel are required to be trained. This includes full-time, part-time, or contractor vessel or company security personnel. The required training includes the provisions of the vessel security plan, and understanding of the Maritime Security (MARSEC) Levels, the Transportation Worker Identification Credential program, as well as recognition of dangerous substances and devices that could be a threat to the vessel.

All of the ship's crew and vessel and company security must receive initial and then annual security training. Vessel security personnel must also receive specialized training related to specific security assignments at the time they are assigned to such functions. Documentation of all security training must be recorded and documented by the vessel security officer.

VESSEL SECURITY ASSESSMENT

In order to develop an adequate vessel security plan and program, a vessel security assessment must be conducted. The goal is to have a secure and safe environment that allows for the normal operations of the vessel and its mission. The vessel security assessment allows the security department to be proactive to criminal activity, piracy, and terrorism rather than reactive. Being proactive reduces risk and should an incident occur it fosters a more positive outcome.

The vessel security assessment is accomplished by conducting a comprehensive review of the security threats and vulnerabilities of the vessel based on the type of vessel, its mission, cargo, and area of operations. Based on the results of this security risk assessment, the size of the security and type of physical security measures can be determined that provide the adequate countermeasures based on the risk and threats to the vessel and crew. Security access control to the ship when at port is vital to reducing the threat to the vessels (see Figure 9.1).

The vessel security assessment is an ongoing process and not just a onetime event. At a minimum, a vessel security assessment needs to be conducted at least once a year. A vessel security assessment is recommended before each deployment at sea and this is even more important that the vessel is traveling into a new and possible hostile area. When a security incident occurs, a review of the incident should be conducted. The purpose is to see how security department and the security plan performed during the incident. This is an excellent opportunity for an updated security assessment.

VESSEL SECURITY PLAN

The vessel security plan is a requirement of the ISPS Code and is based on the vessel security assessment. The required components of the plan include the following security concepts and practices: security measures to prevent unauthorized access onto the vessel as well as to prevent weapons or any other dangerous substances being transported onto the vessel; identification of the vessel security staff such as uniforms and photo identification; procedures to respond effectively to counter criminal

FIGURE 9.1   Controlling access to a ship is vital to reducing a threat. Edinburgh Port, Scotland. (Photograph by Daniel J. Benny.)

activity, piracy, or terrorism threats against the vessel, crew, and cargo based on the MARSEC Levels.

USCG MARSEC Levels

- Level 3—Exceptional: Probable or imminent risk of security incident.
- Level 2—Heightened: Heightened risk of a security incident.
- Level 1—Normal: Normal level of operation for port and vessels.

Other requirements in the plan include procedures to deal with the evaluation of security breaches, security reporting methods, evacuations, security of the cargo, and the facilitation of crew shore leave when docked at ports of call. The vessel security plan should be reviewed on a regular basis and updated as the need requires.

Vessel Security Plan Suggested Outline

- Vessel Security Organization
- Vessel Security Personnel Training
- Exercises and Drills
- Records Management

- Response to MARSEC Levels
- Interaction with Facilities and Other Vessels
- Declarations of Security
- Security Communications
- Physical Security of the Vessel
- Security of Restricted Areas
- Cargo Security
- Security Incidents
- Vessel Security Assessment
- Updating the Vessel Security Plan

PHYSICAL SECURITY AND EQUIPMENT FOR VESSELS

Many of the physical security measures addressed in Chapter 4 of this book can be used on the vessel. This includes locks, access controls, intrusion detection systems, security cameras, security lighting, and some of the physical barriers.

Security equipment specifically related to vessels includes the Automatic Identification Systems (AISs). This system allows for the rapid identification of the ship's identity, type, position, course, speed, navigational status to other shore stations, other ships and aircraft equipped to receive such information.

As stated in SOLAS Resolution XI-2/6, oceangoing vessels in high-risk areas are required to have a Ship Security Alert System. The purpose of this system is to provide protection from piracy and terrorism on the sea by linking the ship's silent alarm to a global satellite system. This beacon transmits a specific country code to the Rescue Coordination Center. This allows the center to dispatch military or law enforcement forces to counter the terrorism or piracy threat. The Global Maritime Distress and Safety System (GMDSS) consists of a network of systems to be used during an emergency of any type.

Other physical security measures can be deployed to prevent unauthorized access to the ship when at sea. This includes the use of high-pressure water or foam hoses that can be directed at approaching small watercraft or individuals attempting access over the gunwale of the ship. Flares, smoke, or a laser gun may also be used to counter an attack on the ship.

DECLARATION OF SECURITY

A Declaration of Security defined by the Safety of Life at Sea Convention is "an agreement reached between a ship and either a port facility or another ship with which it interacts specifying the security measures each will implement." The U.S. Coast Guard states that a Declaration of Security is "an agreement executed between the responsible vessel and Facility Security Officer, or between Vessel Security Officers and the case of a vessel-to-vessel activity, that provides a means for ensuring that all shared security concerns are properly addressed and security will remain in place throughout the time a vessel is moored to the facility or for the duration of a vessel-to-vessel activity respectively."

What this means is if a ship is operating at a higher security level due to cargo or threats to the ship then a port facility or another ship in which it is in operation with can justify the Declaration of Security to ensure the security and safety of the vessel. The ship that makes the Declaration of Security must provide the period of time of the Declaration.

VESSEL SECURITY COMMUNICATIONS

It is vital that ships have an effective two-way communications system to not only deal with the operation of the ship but during the time of emergencies, especially piracy or terrorism incidents. The communications must be able to provide the location of the ship's latitude, longitude, and time.

FIGURE 9.2 Communication is critical between the ship bridge and other areas of the ship. Edinburgh Port, Scotland. (Photograph by Daniel J. Benny.)

VHF radios are the primary means of security communications on ships. The ship's phone or intercom can be used as a backup means of communications. Radio contact must be maintained during all operations and this is even more important during security situations. Within the shipboard, communication is critical between the ship bridge, control room, and all ingress and egress points on the ship. For communications between two ships in port, it must be maintained at all times during security situations (see Figure 9.2). Communications between ships and a port must also be maintained at all times during a security situation.

Private communications such as handheld radios are not authorized for use onboard the ship. This is to prevent interference with the ship's communications or for such equipment to be used for criminal or terrorist activity.

VESSEL SECURITY ADMINISTRATION

It is a requirement of the Vessel Security Officer to keep records of all security-related information and activity. These records can be maintained in hard copy or in electronic format. All security information must be protected from unauthorized access. All electronic-formatted information must be protected from unauthorized access, deletion, destruction, or amendment.

The information that must be kept includes all the reports of security incidents that include criminal activity, piracy, or terrorism. Any security threats to the ship must be documented as well as any change in the MARSEC Level on the ship based on the incident or threat. A ship Declaration of Security and the reason for the Declaration must also be maintained by the Vessel Security Officer.

All information and records related to security training should include the date, location, duration, and subject matter of the training, as well as the details of the persons who attended and passed the program. All security exercises and drills must also be documented that include the date, scenario, and the outcome of the exercises or drills. Any lessons learned or best practices must also be documented. The ship's annual or any periodic security audits and threat assessments must also be documented.

VESSEL EMERGENCY SECURITY DRILLS AND EXERCISES

Vessel emergency security drills and exercises are important in any security environment, and it is just as important, if not more, onboard a ship.

A ship at sea under threat does not have the luxury of a rapid response from local police or emergency services that a land-based environment offers. The ship's security force must take immediate action to thwart the threat. One of the best methods of ensuring a rapid and effective response by a ship's security force is to have frequent security exercises and drills so that all the members of the force will know their role in such an event. It also allows for the honing of the security plan so that changes can be made to enhance the performance during a real security incident.

It is a requirement that security drills and exercises be conducted at least once every 3 months. If a vessel has been inactive, not at sea for a period of time, it must conduct a security drill within 1 week of being in service. The drills and exercises must test all of the components of the ship's security plan and security force.

Security drills and exercises need to be varied in time and location on the ship and type of security situations. It may be a tabletop simulation, a seminar, or a full-scale live drill and exercise. Once each drill or exercise has been completed, it must be evaluated to determine the success of the event. Any positive or negative aspects of the drill or exercise need to be documented. Improvement should be made based on the results of the drills or exercises.

NAVAL VESSEL PROTECTIVE ZONE

Under U.S. Federal law, Title 33, Section 165 of the Code of Federal Regulations, there is a mandated 500-yard Naval Vessel Protection Zone around all the U.S. Naval vessels more than 100 feet in length. When within 500 yards of a Naval vessel, all boaters, both commercial and recreational, shall operate at the minimum speed necessary to maintain a safe course. In addition to these requirements, boaters must comply with all directions given by the Coast Guard or the Naval vessel inside the 500-yard zone. No vessel or person may approach within 100 yards of the Naval vessel unless authorized by the Coast Guard or the U.S. Naval vessel (see Figure 9.3).

Violators of these regulations are subject to civil and/or criminal penalties, including the use of deadly force when necessary, for the safety and security of the Naval vessel.

While a Naval vessel is in transit, the Coast Guard establishes a moving security zone around the vessel. This security zone is in place for the Naval vessel's safety and security.

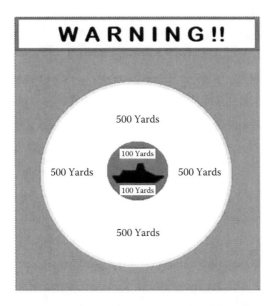

FIGURE 9.3 Naval Vessel Protective Zone; 500 Yards: Minimum Speed, 100 Yards: Do Not Enter. (From the U.S. Navy, Arlington, Virginia.)

BIBLIOGRAPHY

Mid-Atlantic Maritime Academy. (2012). *Vessel security officer.* Virginia Beach, VA: Author.

United States Department of Homeland Security. (2008). *Small vessel security strategy.* Washington, DC: U.S. Government Printing Office.

United States Power Squadron/University of West Florida. (2012). USPS University/University of West Florida Seminar Small Boat Security. Pensacola, FL: University of West Florida.

U.S. Coast Guard America's Waterway Watch Program

America's Waterway Watch is a public outreach program encouraging participants to simply report suspicious activity to the Coast Guard or other law enforcement agencies. Unlike some Neighborhood Watch programs, it is not a formal organization as there are no meetings, membership cards, or membership requirements, and the public does not become an agent of the Coast Guard or any other law enforcement agency.

The program seeks the participation of all members of the maritime community such as towboat operators, recreational boaters, marina operators, or others who live, work, or engage in recreational activity around America's waterways by participating in its America's Waterway Watch program, a nationwide initiative similar to the well-known and successful Neighborhood Watch program that asks community members to report suspicious activities to local law enforcement agencies.

Individuals who spend time on or near the water already know what is normal and what is not, and are well suited to notice suspicious activities possibly indicating threats to U.S. homeland security. Participants in America's Waterway Watch should adopt a heightened sense of awareness toward unusual events or individuals they may encounter in or around ports, docks, marinas, riversides, beaches, or waterfront communities (see Figure 10.1).

FIGURE 10.1   Those who boat in familiar areas should be alert to unusual and suspicious activity. (Photograph by Daniel J. Benny.)

IDENTIFYING SUSPICIOUS ACTIVITY

Watch for suspicious activities of vessels and individuals in locations such as

- Under and around bridges, tunnels, or overpasses
- Near commercial areas or services like ports, fuel docks, cruise ships, or marinas
- Near industrial facilities like power plants and oil, chemical, or water-intake facilities
- Near military bases and vessels, other government facilities, or security zones
- In and around passenger terminals, ferries, and day cruise lines
- Near railroad lines serving any of the aforementioned listed facilities

The public is not expected to patrol any particular area. The public's expertise in recognizing suspicious activity is derived from their familiarity with the surroundings in which they engage in normal work or recreation around the waterfront.

Suspicious activity is a pattern of behavior that arouses a feeling that something is not right. It is important to remember that the behavior of individuals that are suspicious is not based on their ethnic, religious, or national origin.

Identifying suspicious activity starts with understanding the steps a terrorist group takes to plan an attack. The acronym SETS will help one to understand the basic steps and indicators.

Surveillance involves photographing, videotaping, drawing and/or mapping, or other means of monitoring a potential target. (Types of surveillance include fixed, mobile, progressive, creative, overt, and covert.)

Elicitation involves asking detailed questions in an attempt to gain knowledge of hidden or proprietary information. Things to keep in mind include the following.

Listen carefully when engaged in a conversation with a stranger. When he or she begins to ask or inquire about guarded information you may be involved in, you can suspect that elicitation is being used. Remember, the conversation may seem totally innocent.

Avoid becoming a victim of elicitation by sharing proprietary, classified, or guarded information only with those who possess a need to know; without exception. If you suspect that you are being targeted, simply reply to the elicitor's questions with an inquiring question of your own.

Tests of Security is a tool used to develop timelines of authoritative response to a particular incident or occurrence. Staging an incident can be done to determine access vulnerability and/or establish a timeline for later use. Examples include (but are not limited to) the following:

- Bomb threats
- Small fires (trash can/dumpster)
- Abandoned packages

A test of security is likely to occur in close proximity of a potential target or an integral component in the plan to attack a potential target.

Suspicious Behavior is displayed behavior that is out of place or out of character with the environment. Behavior is the key enabler. What activity is the person(s) engaging in that is out of place with the immediate environment (their surroundings)? If the activity is out of character, then that activity may be considered suspicious.

DOCUMENTING AND REPORTING SUSPICIOUS ACTIVITY

First, call the National Response Center at 877-24WATCH. For immediate danger to life or property, call 911, or call the U.S. Coast Guard on Marine Channel 16. Also contact the marine or port faculty security department if possible. *Never* approach someone who may be about to commit a crime. Take some notes, such as the person's appearance, clothing, vehicle license plate, and the type of boat, vehicle, or aircraft involved. Take a picture if possible but keep your distance if the situation seems hostile.

Be specific with details that are reported to authorities. Generalized descriptions and concerns do not provide sufficient information and may not carry the appropriate sense of urgency. All reports should contain if possible the 5 Ws and an H, which means to be able to articulate a majority of the *Who, What, Where, When, Why,* and *How* aspects of what is going on. Try to observe the following:

People	Boats	Vehicles
Color (hair, eyes, skin)	Color (paint, markings, etc.)	Color (paint, markings, etc.)
Year (of birth, approximate age)	Year (of manufacture)	Year (of manufacture)
Make (race, ethnicity)	Make (make and model of boat)	Make (make and model of vehicle)
Body (height, weight, build, etc.)	Body (length, type: cruiser, runabout, PWC)	Body (sedan, truck, SUV, 4/2 door, etc.)
Attire (clothing, description, dress, etc.)	Accessories (name, antennas, flag, inboard/outboard)	Anything else (dents, stickers, rims, etc.)
Looks (hair, scars, tattoos, facial hair, etc.)	License/registration number	License plate number
Sex (male, female)	State of registration	State of registration

AMERICA'S WATERWAY WATCH (AWW) PROGRAM SECURITY RECOMMENDATIONS

Boats should be secured and locked when not onboard. Take the keys. Disable the engine on stored or trailered boats, and make sure the boat cannot be moved easily.

For the manager of a waterside facility where employees such as dockmasters or attendants wear uniforms or safety apparel with identifying logos, badges, and/or nametags, make sure the uniforms are stored in a relatively secure area, which is safe from theft by potential terrorists who may want to blend in by assuming a false identity.

Display an America's Waterway Watch decal prominently on the window of boats or at maritime facilities.

Marinas and other waterfront businesses should display an America's Waterway Watch poster and banners and have informational brochures and decals readily available for customers who want to participate in the

FIGURE 10.2   America's Waterway Watch banner at Long Level Marina, Wrightsville, Pennsylvania. (Photograph by Daniel J. Benny.)

program. A key deterrent to terrorism is publicizing the fact that people are watching for suspicious activity (see Figure 10.2).

For further information about AWW or training on how to identify suspicious activities, contact your local Coast Guard office or a local Flotilla of the Coast Guard Auxiliary. The U.S. Coast Guard or U.S. Coast Guard Auxiliary will be pleased to arrange formal classroom training for all maritime employees as well as promotional and educational information on America's Waterway Watch program.

A Study of America's Waterway Watch Program

The Impact of the U.S. Coast Guard America's Waterway Watch Program on Crime at Pennsylvania Marinas

by
Daniel J. Benny, Ph.D., CPP, PCI, CFE, CCO, CIPM
Private Investigator and Security Consultant 2014

Abstract: As follow-on to the general aviation Aircraft Owners and Pilots Association Marina Watch study, this study examined America's Waterway Watch program to determine if it has been implemented at marinas throughout the Commonwealth of Pennsylvania in an endeavor to prevent and reduce crime in the maritime community. The quantitative research using the Ex-post-facto design was conducted to establish if America's Waterway Watch program where implemented at marinas located in the Commonwealth of Pennsylvania has had an impact on the crime at those marinas. The study's sample included 33 marinas located in the Commonwealth of Pennsylvania. Data were collected by examining the Uniformed Crime Reports in the places where the marinas were located. Data were also collected by the researcher visiting each marina to observe if America's Waterway Watch program was used at the marinas. The purpose of this study was to examine the marinas and determine the effects of America's Waterway Watch program on crime at the marinas that adopted this program during the period from 2010 to 2013.

Introduction

In this study, the maritime community addressed through the U.S. Coast Guard America's Waterway Watch program is a public outreach program encouraging participants to simply report suspicious activity to the Coast Guard or other law enforcement agencies. Unlike some Neighborhood Watch programs it is not a formal organization as there are no meetings, membership cards, or membership requirements. The public does not become an agent of the Coast Guard or any other law enforcement agency.

The goal of the program is to seek the participation of all members of the maritime community such as towboat operators, recreational boaters, marina operators, and individuals who live, work, or engage in recreational activity around America's waterways. Participating in America's Waterway Watch program is similar to the well-known and successful Neighborhood Watch program that asks community members to report suspicious activities to local law enforcement agencies (United States Coast Guard, 2014).

Individuals who spend time on or near the water already know what is normal and what is not and are well suited to notice suspicious activities possibly indicating threats to the U.S. homeland security. Participants in America's Waterway Watch should adopt a heightened sense of awareness toward unusual events or individuals they may encounter in or around ports, docks, marinas, riversides, beaches, or waterfront communities (United States Coast Guard, 2014).

America's Waterway Watch Program Security Recommendations

The following U.S. Coast Guard security procedures are recommended under the program. Boats should be secured and locked when not onboard. Disable the engine on stored or trailered boats, and make sure the boat cannot be moved easily.

For the manager of a waterside facility where employees who wear uniforms or safety apparel with identifying logos, badges, or nametags, make sure the uniforms are stored in a relatively secure area safe from theft by potential terrorists who may want to blend in by assuming a false identity.

Display an America's Waterway Watch decal prominently on the window of boats or at maritime facilities. Marinas and other waterfront businesses should display an America's Waterway Watch poster, and have informational brochures and decals readily available for customers who want to participate in the program. A key deterrent to terrorism is publicizing the fact that people are watching for suspicious activity.

The crimes that may occur at a marina would be crimes against persons, the marina facility, and watercraft located at the marina. Crimes against a person would include any crime that has an impact on the person or victim of the crime who is at the marina. This would include the crimes of murder, rape, robbery, assault, stalking, kidnapping, and harassment. Crimes against marina property only affect the physical structures of the marina. Such crimes would include burglary, theft, arson, and vandalism. The crimes that could be perpetrated against the watercraft located at the marina would include theft of the watercraft, theft of marine avionics, vandalism, or even hijacking (United States Coast Guard, 2014).

Purpose of the Study

The completed research provided a review of America's Waterway Watch program at marinas in the Commonwealth of Pennsylvania. The relationship between America's Waterway Watch program and the crime at the marinas was examined. The purpose of the study was to determine the effects of America's Waterway Watch program on crime at the marinas that adopted this program during the period from 2010 to 2013 using an Ex-post-facto design.

Research Questions and Hypotheses

The research examined and answered the following questions:

Research Question 1

Is there a difference in the number of crimes between marinas that have adopted America's Waterway Watch program and those that have not?

H1. There is a difference in the number of crimes between marinas that adopted America's Waterway Watch program and those that have not.

Ho1. There is no difference in the number of crimes between marinas that adopted America's Waterway Watch program and those that have not.

Research Design

A quantitative statistical methodology was utilized to examine the intervention and the control groups. The intervention group consisted of those marinas that have adopted the watch program and the control group consisted of those marinas that did not adopt the study. The completed research examined two existing groups that have not been manipulated during the study. This is because the manipulation has already occurred at the marinas in the Commonwealth of Pennsylvania who have adopted America's Waterway Watch program and marinas in the Commonwealth of Pennsylvania who have not adopted America's Waterway Watch program. Data were collected by examining the Uniform Crime Reporting reports in the places where the marinas were located. Data were also collected by the researcher who visited the marinas studied to observe if America's Waterway Watch program was implemented or not. This Ex-post-facto design was selected because of the fact that the research explored the impact of the America's Waterway Watch program on the crime at the marinas after the fact. What was researched has already occurred and there is no treatment applied. The Ex-post-facto design can be utilized to examine the possible independent variables that may be apparent in the research and where experimentation is impossible because the events have already taken place.

Data Analysis Procedures

Descriptive statistics were conducted on the demographic data. They were used in this research to convert the raw data collected from the marinas to useful information to determine the impact of America's Waterway Watch program on crime at marinas in the Commonwealth of Pennsylvania.

Results

The dependent variable in the study was whether or not there was a change in crime (against people, property, and watercraft) at the marinas based on the adoption of America's Waterway Watch program. The research shows that between 2010 and 2013 there was a reduction in crime at the marinas that adopted America's Waterway Watch program and an increase in crime at the marinas that did not adopt the program. Crime against people at adopter marinas went down from 5 to 0 and the number of crimes went up at nonadopter marinas from 3 to 6. With regard to crime against property at adopter marinas, the number of crimes went down from 80 to 3 and the number of crimes went up at nonadopter marinas from 45 to 88. Related to crime against watercraft at adopter marinas, the number of crimes went down from 29 to 2 and the number of crimes went up at nonadopter marinas from 4 to 13.

Conclusion

The study shows that the marinas that adopted America's Waterway Watch program had a reduction in crime at the marinas, and there was an increase in crime at the marinas that did not adopt the program. Crime against people at adopter marinas went down and the number of crimes went up at nonadopter marinas. With regard to crime against property at adopter marinas, the number of crimes went down and the number of crimes went up at nonadopter marinas. Related to crime against watercraft at adopter marinas, the number of crimes went down and the number of crimes went up at nonadopter marinas.

The completed research shows that America's Waterway Watch program can be a useful tool for the maritime security community in the Commonwealth of Pennsylvania and across the United States in the reduction of crime and prevention of terrorism.

BIBLIOGRAPHY

International Maritime Organization. (2012). *Guide to maritime security and the ISPS code.* London, UK: International Maritime Organization.

Mid-Atlantic Maritime Academy. (2012). *Vessel security officer.* Virginia Beach, VA: Mid-Atlantic Maritime Academy.

United States Coast Guard. (2002). *Maritime strategy for homeland security.* Washington, DC: U.S. Government Printing Office.

United States Coast Guard. (2014). *United States counter piracy and maritime security action plan.* Washington, DC: U.S. Government Printing Office.

United States Department of Homeland Security. (2008). *Small vessel security strategy.* Washington, DC: U.S. Government Printing Office.

United States Power Squadron/University of West Florida. (2012). *USPS University/University of West Florida Seminar Small Boat Security.* Pensacola, FL: University of West Florida.

Appendix A: United States and Territory Boating Law Enforcement Agencies

Alabama Department of Conservation and Natural Resources
Marine Police Division
64 N Union St, Room 438
Montgomery, AL 36130-1451

Alaska Office of Boating Safety
550 W Seventh Ave, Suite 1380
Anchorage, AK 99501-3561

Arkansas Game and Fish Commission
Boating Administration
2 Natural Resources Dr
Little Rock, AR 72205

American Somoa Department of Public Safety
PO Box 5238
Pago Pago, AS 96799

Arizona Game and Fish Department
Law Enforcement Branch
5000 W Carefree Hwy
Phoenix, AZ 85086-5000

California Div of Boating and Waterways
1 Capitol Mall, Suite 500
Sacramento, CA 95814

Colorado DNR, Parks and Wildlife
13787 S Hwy 85
Littleton, CO 80125

Connecticut Department of Energy and Environmental Protection
Boating Division
PO Box 280
Old Lyme, CT 06371-0280

Delaware DNR and Environmental Control
Division of Fish and Wildlife Enforcement
89 Kings Hwy
Dover, DE 19901

Florida Fish and Wildlife Conservation Commission
620 S Meridian St
Tallahassee, FL 32399-1600

Georgia DNR, Law Enforcement Division
Law Enforcement Section
2070 US Hwy 278 SE
Social Circle, GA 30025

Guam Police Department
Special Programs Section
PO Box 23909
GMF Barrigada, GU 96921

Hawaii Department of Land and Natural Resources
Division of Boating and Ocean Recreation
333 Queen St, Suite 300
Honolulu, HI 96813

Iowa DNR, Conservation and Recreation Division
502 E Ninth St
Wallace State Office Building
Des Moines, IA 50319-0034

Idaho Department of Parks and Recreation
Boating Program
PO Box 83720
Boise, ID 83720-0065

Illinois DNR, Office of Law Enforcement
One Natural Resources Way
Springfield, IL 62702

Indiana DNR, Law Enforcement Division
402 W Washington St, Room W255-D
Indianapolis, IN 46204

Kansas Department of Wildlife and Parks
512 SE 25th Ave
Pratt, KS 67124

Kentucky Division of Law Enforcement
Department of Fish and Wildlife
1 Sportsman's Lane
Frankfort, KY 40601

Lousiana Department of Wildlife and Fisheries
Enforcement Division
PO Box 98000
Baton Rouge, LA 70898-9000

Maine Department of Inland Fisheries and Wildlife
284 State St
Augusta, ME 04333

Maine Department of Marine Resources
State House Station 21
Augusta, ME 04333

Maryland DNR, Natural Resources Police
580 Taylor Ave, Bldg E3
Tawes State Office Building
Annapolis, MD 21401

Massachussets Environmental Police
251 Causeway St, Suite 101
Boston, MA 02114

Michigan DNR, Law Enforcement Division
PO Box 30031
Lansing, MI 48909

Minnesota Department of Natural Resources
500 Lafayette Rd
St Paul, MN 55155

Missouri State Highway Patrol
PO Box 568
Jefferson City, MO 65102-1368

Montana Fish, Wildlife, and Parks
Law Enforcement Division
1420 E Sixth Ave
Helena, MT 59620

Nebraska Game and Parks Commission
Law Enforcement Division
2200 N 33rd St
Lincoln, NE 68503-0370

Nevada Department of Wildlife
Division of Law Enforcement
1100 Valley Rd
Reno, NV 89512-2817

New Hampshire Department of Safety, Division of State Police
Marine Patrol Bureau
31 Dock Rd
Gilford, NH 03249-7629

New Jersey State Police
Marine Services Bureau
PO Box 7068
West Trenton, NJ 08628-0068

New Mexico EMNRD, State Parks Division
Boating Safety and Law Enforcement Bureau
1220 South Saint Francis Drive
Santa Fe, NM 87505

New York Office of Parks, Recreation and Historic Preservation
Marine Services Bureau
Albany, NY 12238-0001

North Carolina Wildlife Resources Commission
Division of Enforcement
1717 Mail Service Center
Raleigh, NC 27699-1717

North Dakota Game and Fish Department
Conservation and Communications Division
100 N Bismarck Expy
Bismarck, ND 58501-5095

Northern Mariana Islands Department of Public Safety
Office of Special Programs
PO Box 500791 CK
Saipan, MP 96950-0791

Ohio DNR, Division of Watercraft
2045 Morse Rd Bldg A
Columbus, OH 43229-6693

Oklahoma Highway Patrol
220 NE 38th Terrace
Oklahoma City, OK 73105

Oregon State Marine Board
PO Box 14145
435 Commercial St NE #400
Salem, OR 97309-5065

Pennsylvania Fish and Boat Commission
PO Box 67000
Harrisburg, PA 17106-7000

Puerto Rico Office of the Navigation Commissioner
PO Box 366147
San Juan, PR 00936

Rhode Island Department of Environmental Management
235 Promenade St
Providence, RI 02908

South Carolina Division of Law Enforcement
PO Box 167
Columbia, SC 29202

South Dakota Department of Game, Fish and Parks
Div of Wildlife
523 E Capitol
Pierre, SD 57501-3182

Tennessee Wildlife Resources Agency
Boating Division
PO Box 40747
Nashville, TN 37204

Texas Parks and Wildlife Department
Law Enforcement Division
4200 Smith School Rd
Austin, TX 78744

U.S. Virgin Islands Department of Planning and Natural Resources
Division of Environmental Enforcement
8100 Lindberg Rd 2nd Floor
St Thomas, VI 00802

Utah Division of State Parks and Recreation
1594 W North Temple, Suite 116
Salt Lake City, UT 84114-6001

Virginia Department of Game and Inland Fisheries
4010 W Broad St
PO Box 11104
Richmond, VA 23230-1104

Vermont Police Marine Division
2777 St George Rd
Williston, VT 05495-7429

Washington, DC Metropolitan Police Department
Harbor Patrol Section
550 Water St SW
Washington, DC 20024

Washington State Parks and Recreation Commission, Boating Programs
1111 Israel Road
PO Box 42650
Olympia, WA 98504-2650

West Virginia Division of Natural Resources
Law Enforcement Section
324 Fourth Ave
South Charleston, WV 25303

Wisconsin DNR, Bureau of Law Enforcement
101 S Webster St
PO Box 7921
Madison, WI 53707-7921

Wyoming Game and Fish Department
5400 Bishop Blvd
Cheyenne, WY 82006-0001

Appendix B: Security, Maritime Security, and Boating Organizations

ASIS International
    1625 Prince Street
    Alexandria, VA 22314-2882
    Telephone: 703-519-6200
    E-mail: asis@asisonline.org
    Website: https://www.asisonline.org

Boat US
    880 South Pickett Street
    Alexandria, VA 22304-4605
    Telephone: 703-461-2878
    Website: http://www.boatus.com

International Association for Counterterrorism and Security Professionals
    PO Box 100688
    Arlington, VA 22210
    Telephone: 671-216-8205
    E-mail: iacsp@aol.com
    Website: http://www.iacsp.com

International Association of Maritime Security Professionals
    Kensington High Street 219
    Kensington, London W* 6BD
    London, England
    Telephone: 44(0) 2071933873
    Website: http://iamsponline.org

United States Coast Guard
2703 Martin Luther King Jr. Ave SE
Washington, DC 20593-7000
Telephone: 202-372-2316
Website: http://www.uscg.mil

United States Coast Guard Auxiliary
2703 Martin Luther King Jr. Ave SE
Washington, DC 20593-7000
Telephone: 202-372-2316
Website: http://www.cgaux.org

United States Power Squadron
1504 Blue Ridge Road
Raleigh, NC 27607
Telephone: 888-367-8777
Website: http://usps.org

Appendix C: Security, Maritime Security, and Boating Publications

Boat US Magazine
Boat US
880 South Pickett Street
Alexandria, VA 22304-4605
Telephone: 703-461-2878
E-mail: Membership@BoatUS.com
Website: http://www.boatus.com

Coast Guard Journal of Safety & Security at Sea
United States Coast Guard
2703 Martin Luther King Jr. Ave SE
Washington, DC 20593-7000
Telephone: 202-372-2316
Website: http://www.uscg.mil

Journal of Counterterrorism and Homeland Security International
International Association for Counterterrorism and Security Professionals
PO Box 100688
Arlington, VA 22210
Telephone: 671-216-8205
E-mail: iacsp@aol.com
Website: http://www.iacsp.com

Maritime Security International
Suite 24/25
Hurlingham Studios, Ranelagh Gardens
London SW6 3PA, United Kingdom
Telephone: +44(0) 207386 6100
E-mail: inbox@mar-media.com
Website: www.maritimesecurityinternational.net

Navigator
  United States Coast Guard Auxiliary
  1301 First Street, Suite E. Rivers Edge
  Granite City, IL 62040

Security Management
  ASIS International
  1625 Prince Street
  Alexandria, VA 22314-2882
  Telephone: 703-519-6200
  E-mail: asis@asisonline.org
  Website: https://www.asisonline.org

Appendix D: U.S. Piracy Laws

TITLE 18: CRIMES AND CRIMINAL PROCEDURE

PART I: Crimes

Chapter 81: Piracy and Privateering

Table of Contents:

SEC. 1651. PIRACY UNDER LAW OF NATIONS

Whoever, on the high seas, commits the crime of piracy as defined by the law of nations, and is afterward brought into or found in the United States, shall be imprisoned for life.

SEC. 1652. CITIZENS AS PIRATES

Whoever, being a citizen of the United States, commits any murder or robbery, or any act of hostility against the United States, or against any citizen thereof, on the high seas, under color of any commission from any foreign prince, or state, or on pretense of authority from any person, is a pirate, and shall be imprisoned for life.

SEC. 1653. ALIENS AS PIRATES

Whoever, being a citizen or subject of any foreign state, is found and taken on the sea making war upon the United States, or cruising against the vessels and property thereof, or of the citizens of the same, contrary to the provisions of any treaty existing between the United States and the state of which the offender is a citizen or subject, when by such treaty such acts are declared to be piracy, is a pirate, and shall be imprisoned for life.

SEC. 1654. ARMING OR SERVING ON PRIVATEERS

Whoever, being a citizen of the United States, without the limits thereof, fits out and arms, or attempts to fit out and arm or is concerned in furnishing, fitting out, or arming any private vessel of war or privateer, with an intent that such vessel shall be employed to cruise or commit hostilities upon the citizens of the United States or their property; or

Whoever takes the command of or enters on board of any such vessel with such an intent; or

Whoever purchases any interest in any such vessel with a view to share in the profits thereof—

Shall be fined under this title or imprisoned not more than 10 years, or both.

SEC. 1655. ASSAULT ON COMMANDER AS PIRACY

Whoever, being a seaman, lays violent hands upon his commander, to hinder and prevent his fighting in defense of his vessel or the goods entrusted to him, is a pirate, and shall be imprisoned for life.

SEC. 1656. CONVERSION OR SURRENDER OF VESSEL

Whoever, being a captain or other officer or mariner of a vessel upon the high seas or on any other waters within the admiralty and maritime jurisdiction of the United States, piratically or feloniously runs away with such vessel, or with any goods or merchandise thereof, to the value of $50 or over; or

Whoever yields up such vessel voluntarily to any pirate—Shall be fined under this title or imprisoned not more than 10 years, or both.

SEC. 1657. CORRUPTION OF SEAMEN AND CONFEDERATING WITH PIRATES

Whoever attempts to corrupt any commander, master, officer, or mariner to yield up or to run away with any vessel, or any goods, wares, or merchandise, or to turn pirate or to go over to or confederate with pirates, or in any wise to trade with any pirate, knowing him to be such; or

Whoever furnishes such pirate with any ammunition, stores, or provisions of any kind; or

Whoever fits out any vessel knowingly and, with a design to trade with, supply, or correspond with any pirate or robber upon the seas; or

Whoever consults, combines, confederates, or corresponds with any pirate or robber upon the seas, knowing him to be guilty of any piracy or robbery; or

Whoever, being a seaman, confines the master of any vessel— Shall be fined under this title or imprisoned not more than three years, or both.

SEC. 1658. PLUNDER OF DISTRESSED VESSEL

Whoever plunders, steals, or destroys any money, goods, merchandise, or other effects from or belonging to any vessel in distress, or wrecked, lost, stranded, or cast away, upon the sea, or upon any reef, shoal, bank, or rocks of the sea, or in any other place within the admiralty and maritime jurisdiction of the United States, shall be fined under this title or imprisoned not more than 10 years, or both.

Whoever willfully obstructs the escape of any person endeavoring to save his life from such vessel, or the wreck thereof; or

Whoever holds out or shows any false light, or extinguishes any true light, with an intent to bring any vessel sailing upon the sea into danger or distress or shipwreck—

Shall be imprisoned not less than 10 years and may be imprisoned for life.

SEC. 1659. ATTACK TO PLUNDER VESSEL

Whoever, upon the high seas or other waters within the admiralty and maritime jurisdiction of the United States, by surprise or open force, maliciously attacks or sets upon any vessel belonging to another, with an intent unlawfully to plunder the same, or to despoil any owner thereof of any moneys, goods, or merchandise laden on board thereof, shall be fined under this title or imprisoned not more than 10 years, or both.

SEC. 1660. RECEIPT OF PIRATE PROPERTY

Whoever, without lawful authority, receives or takes into custody any vessel, goods, or other property, feloniously taken by any robber or pirate against the laws of the United States, knowing the same to have been feloniously taken, shall be imprisoned not more than 10 years.

SEC. 1661. ROBBERY ASHORE

Whoever, being engaged in any piratical cruise or enterprise, or being of the crew of any piratical vessel, lands from such vessel and commits robbery on shore, is a pirate, and shall be imprisoned for life.

Appendix E: U.S. Navy Physical Security at Private Contractor's Facilities

U.S. Navy Physical Security at Private Contractor's Facilities

SCOPE

Title: Physical Security at Private Contractor's Facility; accomplish

REFERENCES

33 CFR Part 165, Regulated Navigation Areas and Limited Access Areas

33 CFR Part 334, Danger Zone and Restricted Area Regulations

REQUIREMENTS

3.1 The requirements of 3.2.5, 3.2.6, 3.2.7, 3.2.8, and 3.2.9 are Force Protection measures the Contractor shall be able to meet under Force Protection Conditions Normal, Alpha, Bravo, Charlie, and Delta, respectively. The solicitation shall define the Force Protection Condition.

Implementation of any other measures, when directed by the SUPERVISOR, will be the subject of an equitable adjustment.

Provide a written plan which shall be implemented for the protection of personnel, U.S. Naval vessels, work in process, the material and equipment to be installed therein, and GFM dry docks (as applicable) at the Contractor's facility, which addresses the requirements of this Standard Item. The written plan shall, as a minimum, be identified as "For Official Use Only (FOUO)."

Provide written designation to the SUPERVISOR of the individual who will be in charge of the security effort.

Attend security coordination meeting with Ship's Force and the SUPERVISOR to brief the Contractor's security plan and procedures prior to security conference of 3.2.3.

Conduct a security conference with federal, state, and local authorities, Ship's Force, and the SUPERVISOR within 45 calendar days prior to ship's arrival to ensure all parties are in agreement with the security procedures while the ship is in port.

Coordinate the establishment of the land and water areas adjacent to U.S. Naval vessels as restricted areas or limited waterway areas in accordance with 2.1 or 2.2, in cooperation with the Navy, U.S. Coast Guard, and Army Corps of Engineers.

Under Force Protection Condition NORMAL, establish and maintain physical security boundaries, positive access controls, and other security measures to provide safeguards against hazards, including unauthorized entry, malicious mischief, theft, espionage, sabotage, and terrorism at Contractor's facility in accordance with Attachment A, to include the following:

perimeter physical barriers
perimeter openings control
access and circulation control
armed security force
protective lighting
signs and posting of boundaries
security force communications
random antiterrorism measures (RAM)

Under Force Protection Condition ALPHA, establish and maintain the following requirements in addition to 3.2.5:

additional plant boundary protection.
assistance from state, local, and other law enforcement agencies.
increased personnel, property, and perimeter security checks.
increased security force manning commensurate with the additional actions directed under this section.
increased waterfront surveillance.
place vehicle barriers to reduce ease of vehicular access adjacent to the ship.
brief the security force and the SUPERVISOR concerning the threat, the security precautions being implemented, and what action is to be taken with respect to strangers, unidentified vehicles, abandoned parcels or suitcases, or unusual activity in or near the Contractor's facility.

increase security spot checks of vehicles, persons, and buildings near U.S. Naval vessels.

limit access points for vehicles and personnel commensurate with performance of the Job Order.

inspect 100% of commercial vehicles entering the controlled industrial area and/or piers.

test procedures for mass notification.

review requirements related to implementing additional security actions in the event of an increased threat.

review barrier plans.

Under Force Protection Condition BRAVO, establish and maintain the following requirements in addition to 3.2.5 through 3.2.6:

request the captain of the Port or U.S. Coast Guard District Commander to activate the Naval Vessel Protection Zones in accordance with 2.1.

establish communications with state, local, and other law enforcement, fire, and emergency management agencies.

at the beginning of each workday, as well as at random intervals, inspect the interior and exterior of buildings in regular use for suspicious packages. Secure and regularly inspect buildings, rooms, and storage areas not in regular use for unusual conditions or suspicious activity.

clear the area within 100 feet (30.5 m) of U.S. Naval vessels of all non-mission-essential materials and vehicles as determined by the SUPERVISOR.

review requirements related to implementing additional security actions in the event of an increasing threat.

identify paths for critical materials to maintain production

brief all employees working at the facility, including the ship's crew and subcontractor employees, concerning the threat, the security precautions being implemented, and what action is to be taken with respect to strangers, unidentified vehicles, abandoned parcels, containers or suitcases, and any other suspicious or unusual activity.

increase security presence and surveillance, and randomly inspect vehicles, persons, and accompanying items entering the facility.

review mail and material screening procedures at the facility.

Under Force Protection Condition CHARLIE, establish and maintain the following requirements in addition to 3.2.5 through 3.2.7:

inspect the interior and exterior of buildings in regular use for suspicious activity or objects at frequent intervals.

increase protection for crew berthing to reduce vulnerability.

list work that would be required to permit safe relocation of the vessel and its crew to the nearest Government facility as designated by the SUPERVISOR.

determine work that will be stopped if the next higher Force Protection Condition is implemented. Determine a list of and inform mission-essential personnel, including Contractor work force. Communicate critical Work Items to the SUPERVISOR, ship's Commanding Officer, and/or Shipyard Commander.

increase surveillance in and around waterside perimeter and facilities. Position floats, work boats, and barges along the sides of the U.S. Naval vessel and any occupied berthing barges to create a buffer zone.

limit access points to strictly enforce entry control. Inspect all vehicles entering the controlled industrial area and/or pier. Review access procedures to ensure no unauthorized personnel gain access into the facility.

Under Force Protection Condition DELTA, establish and maintain the following requirements in addition to 3.2.5 through 3.2.8:

immediately notify state and local law enforcement agencies and the U.S. Coast Guard of any knowledge of terrorist activity, suspicious persons, or criminal activity.

limit access points to the absolute minimum.

strictly control all facility access points, ensure positive identification of all personnel, and search all vehicles and their contents, suitcases, briefcases, and packages entering the Contractor's facility.

accomplish continuous security patrols of all areas of the facility, to include the waterfront, occupied by U.S. Naval vessels and personnel.

prepare U.S. Naval vessels for movement away from the Contractor's facility when directed by the SUPERVISOR.

discontinue work except that directly related to the integrity of the vessel and as otherwise directed by the SUPERVISOR.

implement the plan to deny access to individuals not essential or critical to the overall mission of protecting and/or moving vital Navy assets onto the facility and occupied buildings.

Submit one legible copy, in approved transferable media, of the plan to the SUPERVISOR for review and approval no later than 15 days prior to availability start date.

Accomplish the requirements of the approved plan.

Any changes at the Contractor's facility affecting physical security or the approved plan shall be submitted to the SUPERVISOR for approval within 24 hours.

Provide procedures for coordinating the Contractor's security efforts with those of the SUPERVISOR and the Commanding Officer's designated representative.

Prepare an itemized statement of cost incurred for the work covered by this Standard Item. Submit one legible copy, in approved transferable media, of the statement to the SUPERVISOR within 30 days of delivery or redelivery (as applicable) of the ship. The statement shall itemize the total direct labor hours with the applicable direct labor rates, overhead, General and Administrative (G&A) and/or other indirect rates, material, material handling charges, subcontractor costs, Other Direct Costs (ODC), and freight costs (as applicable). Where final overhead rates are not available, use the most current billing rate(s).

The Government may perform an audit of the Contractor's statement of cost incurred. The Contractor, upon request, shall make available to the SUPERVISOR all records, related correspondence, and the substantiating data upon which the statement of cost incurred is based.

NOTES

U.S. Naval vessel means any vessel owned, operated, chartered, or leased by the U.S. Navy; any pre-commissioned vessel under construction for the U.S. Navy, once launched into the water; and any vessel under the operational control of the U.S. Navy or a Combatant Command.

Controlled Industrial Area (CIA) means an area of the shipyard in which construction, conversion, repair, or overhaul of U.S. Navy vessels is conducted.

USFF AT OPORD 3300 (series) provides general security requirements for Fleet Activities. The SUPERVISOR will use this reference as a guide in applying force protection measures appropriate to the unique situation at each Contractor's facility.

A vehicle is defined as a means of transportation that transports people or objects.

ATTACHMENT A: OTHER SECURITY MEASURES

Perimeter Physical Barriers

Physical barriers, including both natural (e.g., mountains, swamps, thick vegetation, rivers, bays, cliffs) and structural (e.g., fences, walls, doors, gates, vehicle barriers) which control, delay, impede, and discourage access by unauthorized persons. To be effective, such barriers shall be augmented by armed security force personnel or other means of protection and assessment.

Physical barriers shall be employed along Contractor's facility perimeters. The barrier or combination of barriers used shall afford an equal degree of continuous protection along the entire perimeter.

Structural barriers such as fences or walls shall be a minimum of 8 feet in height, and any uncontrolled opening shall be securable to afford protection against unauthorized entry.

The waterfront security required to protect the Navy asset is dependent on the asset.

Closed-circuit television (CCTV) installs will be planned for installation by using Chapter 4 of the Unified Facilities Criteria (UFC) 4-021-02NF. Plans will be submitted to the SUPERVISOR for approval, prior to installation. This UFC document provides guidance on how to design electronic security systems required by the current antiterrorism/force-protection environment.

The patent number for the original Port Security Barrier (PSB) is 6,681,709 B1. The patent number for the Port Security Barrier–T variant (PSB-T) is 7,401,565 B2. There is no separate patent for the Port Security Barrier–V variant (PSB-V). At the time of publishing SI 009-72 FY-12 (CH-2), Harbor Offshore Barriers (5720 Nicolle St., Ventura, CA 93003) and Truston Technologies, Inc. (520 Ridgely Ave., Annapolis, MD 21401) were both licensed to manufacture the original PSB, as well as both the T and V variant.

Asset	Security Measures
For Patrol Coastal (PC), MSC Strategic Sealift Ship (SSS) (reduced operational status)	Adjacent landside security (patrols, surveillance, pier access control) no special requirements in waterways.
	Identify restricted area waterways with buoys and signs.
Surface combatants, Amphibious ships (full operational status), auxiliary, MSCSSS, ammunition ships, mine warfare	The aforementioned requirements and
	Security Zone per 3.2.4
	Use of a Port Security Barrier (PSB-V or -T model dependent on expected geographic and environmental conditions as determined by the SUPERVISOR) per 1.d mentioned earlier, or other physical barrier approved by the numbered Fleet commander.

(Continued)

Asset	Security Measures
	In areas where the cognizant SUPERVISOR agrees the use of waterborne barrier(s) is not in the best interest of the U.S. Navy, a dedicated waterborne security boat shall patrol within 200 yards of the protected vessel equipped with a bullhorn, night vision device, spotlight, marine flares, lethal and non-lethal weapons, and a two-way communications device according to the specifications described in Addendum 1.
	**Note: If PSB-V or -T or SUPERVISOR authorized (numbered Fleet commander-approved) physical barrier is in place, a dedicated waterborne security asset is not required.
Carriers, submarines (see next row for SSBN)	The aforementioned requirements and
	Electronic water/waterside security system to include, but not limited to, closed-circuit television for the purposes of surface craft detection.
	Use water barriers to prevent direct unchallenged access from small boat attacks.
SSBN	The aforementioned requirements and
	Per SECNAVINST S8126.1
	Use water barriers to stop small boat threat

Perimeter Openings

Openings in the perimeter barrier shall be kept to the minimum necessary for the safe and efficient operation of the Contractor's facility. Access through such openings shall be controlled, or the openings shall be secured.

Access and Circulation Control

A system of personnel and vehicle movement control is required at Contractor's facilities. The degree of control shall be in keeping with efficient operations yet afford defense in depth to provide graduated levels of protection.

Armed or unarmed sentries may be assigned to check identification at pedestrian and vehicle entry control points to restrict and control movement by vehicles and unauthorized personnel from gaining access into the facility.

The facility shall coordinate with the local postal and courier services in developing a plan for ensuring that all mail and courier delivered packages to the facility are properly screened by the delivery service prior to being delivered to the Contractor facility's mailroom.

Armed Security Force

The Contractor security force shall consist of designated persons specifically organized, trained, armed, and equipped to provide physical security.

Protective Lighting

Protective lighting, such as work lighting, increases the effectiveness of security forces and has considerable deterrent value.

Contractors shall provide adequate illumination to discourage or detect attempts to enter facilities and reveal the presence of unauthorized persons within such areas.

Lighting shall support security force activities such as identification of badges and personnel at perimeter openings, surveillance of facility perimeter/avenues of approach, and inspection of unusual or suspicious circumstances.

Signs and Posting of Boundaries

Trespass laws applicable to the jurisdiction in which the facility is located will govern signs and posting of perimeter boundaries at Contractor's facilities.

Size, placement, and use of any language in addition to English should be appropriate for the stated purpose. Signs will read essentially as follows:

WARNING

RESTRICTED AREA

KEEP OUT

Authorized Personnel Only

Signs shall be posted at regularly used points of entry and at intervals along the facility perimeter such that any reasonable person would conclude that everyone crossing the boundary into the facility would have been informed of the aforementioned signs.

Security Force Communications

The activity security force requires sufficient equipment to maintain continuous, secure two-way voice communications between elements (fixed/mobile posts, and supervisory personnel) of the security force and U.S. Naval vessel's watch section. Establish communications between the Contractor's security force and the U.S. Naval vessel's watch section.

The facility shall maintain a communication system for use in emergencies or crisis situations to facilitate effective two-way voice communications among state and local law enforcement agencies and the U.S. Coast Guard.

The facility shall establish a communication system, pre-recorded and/or live-voice, but capable of broadcasting information to all building occupants or personnel in the immediate vicinity during or prior to an emergency or crisis situation.

Random Antiterrorism Measures (RAM)

As a deterrent, randomly apply the measures from higher Force Protection Conditions and other RAM including the following:

keep personnel involved in implementing increased security requirements on call.

inspect deliveries to protect against the introduction of unauthorized material.

cars and other non-mission essential items shall be moved 100 feet from U.S. Naval vessels and buildings where the crew is located or work is in progress.

inspect mail for letter or parcel bombs.

on entry of visitors to the facility, physically inspect them and accompanying items.

search vehicles entering the facility.

erect barriers and obstacles to provide additional traffic controls to areas where U.S. Naval vessels and crews are located.

consult local authorities about closing public roads and facilities that might make sites more vulnerable.

other site-specific RAM that shall be incorporated into the Contractor's physical security plan and/or company-specific implementation procedures.

ADDENDUM ONE TO ATTACHMENT A
OF STANDARD ITEM 009-72

Waterborne Security Boats

Mission

The boats are primarily used to provide a dedicated waterborne presence and deterrence in the immediate vicinity of no more than three (3) U.S. Naval Assets. The word "dedicated" is defined as on-site, 24 hours a day, 7 days a week, and responsive solely to the operational confines of the protected asset(s). Normally, a single waterborne security boat will be designated for each U.S. Naval Asset. Waterborne security boats must be capable of conducting continuous patrols in the immediate vicinity of the protected asset(s), or continuous monitoring of a patrol zone when assigned to protect clustered U.S. Naval Assets (a patrol zone shall not exceed 200 yards and shall not include more than three protected assets).

Waterborne security boats will be used to provide restricted area enforcement by providing a layered defense and deterrence mechanism. This includes the ability for early detection of intruders under day/night, and all-weather conditions.

Projected Operating Environment

The projected operating environment of the waterborne security boats will normally be in protected harbors or inland waterways. These boats will be expected to operate in varying temperatures depending on the climate at the location the boat(s) will be used. Temperatures can be expected to vary from below 32°F to above 100°F. Storm conditions and warnings often issued in the operating environment include small craft, gale, storm, and hurricane warnings.

General Characteristics

There are no specific hull material requirements for waterborne security boats. Waterborne security boats must be visible from distances of at least 500 yards to the unaided eye, during periods of unrestricted visibility and must possess all safety equipment required by federal and local regulations. Waterborne security boats must also display a placard on both sides of the vessel with the word "Security" of sufficient size and reflective composition to be visible from 500 yards to the unaided eye, during periods of unrestricted visibility (250 yards during periods of low light) and in accordance with federal and local regulations. These boats must possess a hailing mechanism capable of warning/hailing approaching craft at 500 yards. Hailing capability may consist of modified human voice (e.g., through the use of a bull horn, PA system, etc.), or mechanical (e.g., siren, pulsating tone, etc.).

The boat must have a weather-resistant spot/floodlight capable of rotating 360° with instant start/restart and at least 6,000,000 candlepower.

The boat must have a fully operable marine band radio (VHF).

Length range: 27–40 feet And why:

This size is necessary for safety and mission accomplishment, ease of discernment, crew accommodation, visual deterrent, and ease of maneuverability when responding to contacts of interest during all-weather patrols.

Breadth: 8 feet 6 inches And why:

The minimum breadth of 8 feet 6 inches is necessary to provide a stable platform, crew accommodation, visual deterrent, ease of maneuverability, safety, and mission accomplishment when responding to contacts of interest during all-weather patrols.

Maximum Draft: 4.5 feet. The maximum draft of 4.5 feet is necessary for ease of maneuverability in and around the protected assets.

Number of Crew: Two. At least one coxswain and one observer/lookout shall be assigned to each boat for the duration of the patrol period. These personnel shall be qualified in the operation of the security boat and shall be qualified with and armed with personal protective weapons in accordance with SECNAVINST 5500.29C, DoDD 5210.56, and relevant state and local regulations.

Required Cargo Capacity or Deck Space: Stowage space must be sufficient to accommodate at least four (including two spare) life vests, a floodlight, a first aid kit, a backboard, and specialized tactical equipment.

Propulsion System (e.g., diesel inboard with outdrive, diesel inboard with waterjet, or gasoline outboard) and why:

The propulsion system must be able to conduct multiple idle/sprint missions during each patrol period. Because of the limited operating area, propulsion systems must be capable of rapidly responding to a contact of interest (normally within the 200-yard operating zone) and rapidly reversing.

Speed 20 kts. A minimum speed of 20 kts is necessary to provide the capability to rapidly respond to contacts of interest or rapidly move out of the line of fire from shipboard responders in the event of a deadly engagement.

Index